EXPANDING READING SKILLS

•intermediate

Linda Markstein
Louise Hirasawa

NEWBURY HOUSE PUBLISHERS, Inc.
Rowley, Massachusetts 01969
ROWLEY • LONDON • TOKYO

Library of Congress Cataloging in Publication Data

Markstein, Linda.
    Expanding reading skills, intermediate.

    Summary: Presents selections from magazines,
newspapers, and other sources designed to
strengthen reading skills including speed.
Suitable for group instruction as well as self-
instruction.
    1. English language--Text-books for foreigners.
2. Readers--1950-   . [1. Readers. 2. English
language--Textbooks for foreigners] I. Hirasawa,
Louise. II. Title.
PE1128.M346   428.6'4   82-2209
ISBN 0-88377-242-6   AACR2

Cover and book design adapted from that by Harry Swanson.

NEWBURY HOUSE PUBLISHERS, INC.

Language Science
Language Teaching
Language Learning

ROWLEY, MASSACHUSETTS 01969
ROWLEY ● LONDON ●TOKYO

First printing: April 1982

Printed in the U.S.A.   5   4   3   2

TABLE OF CONTENTS

Dedicated to Pat Rooney and to Hermina and Harry Montag

ACKNOWLEDGMENTS

Many people have helped us with *Developing Reading Skills: Intermediate* and *Expanding Reading Skills: Intermediate*. Teachers from New York to China have tested the materials and given us their advice; hundreds and hundreds of students have used the materials, and they have shown us what was good—and what needed to be better. We want to give special thanks to Linda Barker, Gay Brookes, Allan Dart, Barbara Gonzales, Janis Jones, Steve Rooney, and Dorothy and David Seevers. We also want to thank Elizabeth Lantz, Lori Thibodeau, and Jackie Sanborn at Newbury House. Most of all, we want to thank our patient, long-suffering husbands, Katsushige and Steve, and Linda's daughters, Anne and Suzy, who have gone without when deadlines drew nigh. Thank you, all of you. We couldn't have done it without you.

Linda Markstein
The Borough of Manhattan Community College
The City University of New York
New York, New York

Louise Hirasawa
The University of Washington
Seattle, Washington

INTRODUCTION

Expanding Reading Skills: Intermediate is designed for adults who want to strengthen their reading skills for academic, personal, or career purposes. These materials have been tested successfully with both native and non-native speakers of English.

Expanding Reading Skills: Intermediate is part of a reading series by the same authors. It is comparable in difficulty with *Developing Reading Skills: Intermediate,* and it can be used as (a) a replacement or (b) a follow-up for that book. With the possibility of sequence in mind, the authors have taken care to avoid duplication of exercise items in the two texts.

Expanding Reading Skills: Intermediate and *Developing Reading Skills: Intermediate* can also be followed by the advanced texts by the same authors, *Expanding Reading Skills: Advanced* and *Developing Reading Skills: Advanced.*

All the texts in this reading series emphasize reading practice and the development of reading speed. The readings come from current nonfiction magazine and newspaper writing, and they cover a wide subject range in order to expose the reader to the content demands of different types of reading material.

We have tried to select the readings with great care so that we would have to make as few changes as possible from the original texts. Where adaptations (simplifying structures and vocabulary and glossing) were needed, we have relied on the advice of the experts: ESL students and ESL classroom teachers. Their suggestions in extensive field testing have helped us develop materials that are challenging and yet accessible to intermediate-level students.

The readings are arranged in order of difficulty according to field testing. The exercises deliberately build upon vocabulary and structures introduced in earlier chapters, so we recommend that the chapters be presented in the given order if possible.

Suggestions for Introducing the Reading

The more time spent introducing the reading, the better the results. Intermediate-level students in particular benefit from careful reading preparation because it helps them to be more receptive to the content. There are many ways of working into the reading depending upon the goals of the lesson and the needs of the students. In general, we suggest activities of two basic types:

Type A—Content Predictions

1) *Illustrations and Title Clues:* Using only illustrative material (photograph, map, graph) and the title, have the students discuss (a) what they think the subject is; (b) what the picture tells them about the subject; (c) how they feel about the subject, taking care to examine in detail their past experience or knowledge of the subject.

2) *Discussion Topics:* Near the end of every chapter, there are several discussion-composition topics relating to the reading. It can be interesting and useful to give these topics to the students *before* they read the article now and then. This helps to activate their awareness of the subject and gives them a focus for their reading.

3) *Content Expectations:* Ask the students what they expect the article to say before they read it. (Note: It is useful to write these statements on the chalkboard so that they can be re-examined later.)

4) *Point of View:* Ask the students how they think the writer feels about the subject. What view do they expect that he or she will present? Why?

A note of caution: It is quite natural for people to feel hesitant about hazarding these guesses at first. Care has to be taken to establish an environment of freedom where there is no penalty for being "wrong."

Type B—Word Connotation and Tone

In order to develop an awareness of word connotation and word tone, it can be both useful and challenging to focus on activities of another type. These activities we usually introduce with a word-phrase association. We choose a very general, comprehensive word or phrase related to the reading, write it on the chalkboard, and then ask the students to freely associate any words that come to mind until there are perhaps 30 to 40 words and phrases on the board. Some of the activities available at this point are:

1) *Categorizing:* Have the students make up a few general categories into which these words can be classified.

2) *Word Selection:* Have the students (a) decide which words have negative connotations and which ones positive; (b) choose three words they would like to delete; (c) choose the three words they think are most closely related to the subject. Ask them to explain the reasons for their choices.

Because these activities often generate lively discussion and disagreement, it can be useful to have the students work together in small groups.

There are many more ways to extend these introductory activities to suit the needs of a specific class. Above all, we urge you to vary your approach from time to time to heighten student interest and involvement.

Using the Reading Text to Reinforce Other Language Development Activities

In many English as a Foreign Language and English as a Second Language programs, reading is taught in combination with other language-development activities. Consequently, teachers often ask us how our texts can be used to reinforce grammar, sentence structure, and composition activities. We believe that intellectual content is an essential component of real language activities no matter what they may be, and our readers provide content that can be effectively used for a variety of purposes.

Let us suppose that the grammar focus in a lesson is the past tense. Most of the readings in this book can be discussed using past tense:
- *What were some of the reasons the author gave for the expanding deserts?*
- *What were some of the myths about the American family?*
- *What were some of the differences the author mentioned between Mexican and American comic books?*

In the discussion-composition topics near the end of each chapter, we have tried to phrase the topics in such a way as to naturally elicit different verb tenses. These topics may give you ideas for how to focus discussions in order to give practice in specific grammar elements.

If the aim of the lesson is to give practice in pronunciation and intonation, sentences from the reading (or perhaps the comprehension check) can be used. This can lend meaning to the practice.

The readings can be used very easily to teach sentence patterns—and to prove that the various sentence patterns of English are actually used! All the readings provide repeated examples of the sentence patterns.

We have always believed that reading should be taught together with composition and that the best results come from developing these skills together: good readers are good writers are good readers. . . . We have tried to provide interesting, fully developed composition topics in order to guide students in their compositions. These composition topics have proved particularly effective when the students have been given ample opportunity to discuss them before they begin writing.

Reading-Skills Development—Suggested Procedures

The reading class should be one in which students will develop useful reading skills. As in the development of any other skill, guided practice over an extended period of time is essential. In the beginning, many students will have difficulty in finishing the articles in the time you suggest, and they will need encouragement and reassurance from you. (Note: in this text—unlike *Developing Reading Skills: Advanced* and *Expanding Reading Skills: Advanced*—we have not recommended specific reading times. We have given reading speeds (words per minute) after every reading. You can choose the most appropriate time limit for your class. We found too much variation between classes to feel confident about recommending times.)

The students must learn to stop reading word by word and, instead, read to grasp the general ideas of the article. This can be achieved by careful and consistent use of the rapid reading and comprehension exercises. The transition from specific words to general ideas takes time, and the students need a great deal of encouragement to make this adjustment. They should try to guess the probable meanings of unfamiliar words from their contexts rather than look these words up in the dictionary. (We recommend that dictionaries not be used at all in the classroom.)

The Comprehension Check reflects the major ideas of the article in order to help the students learn to focus on important information. When they read the article a second time, they will be aware, through the Check statements, of what information is important, and they should be encouraged to read with these statements in mind. The Check statements appear in the same order as the presentation of relevant information in the article to aid in recall of that information and to develop a sense of the article's organization.

Expanding Reading Skills: Intermediate has been designed for self-instruction as well as for class instruction (a separate answer key is available). When the text is used for self-instruction, the student will achieve the best results by following the recommended reading procedures.

The rapid reading must be carefully controlled to be effective. We recommend the following steps and suggest that the entire first lesson be done carefully in class to make sure everyone understands the procedure.

1) The students should write the numbers 1 through 10 on both sides of a piece of paper, marking one side "Test 1" and the other side "Test 2."
2) The teacher then announces the amount of time for the first reading of the article. (Note: the time should be limited enough to provide challenge.) Students begin reading.
3) While the students are reading, they should be told at intervals how many minutes they have left and which paragraph they should be starting: for example, "Four minutes, paragraph seven." If a timer clock is used, they can pace themselves.
4) When the teacher announces "Time is up!" the students *must* stop reading whether or not they have finished the article. (In the beginning, many students may *not* finish the article on the first reading.)

5) Students should turn to the Comprehension Check at the end of the chapter, read the statements, and answer true (T) or false (F) on their papers under Test 1. The students should base their answers *only* on information contained in the article.

6) When they have completed the Comprehension Check, students should turn their papers over so that Test 1 answers cannot be seen.

7) The teacher should ask the students to reread the article, *starting from the beginning* and skimming quickly over previously read portions.

8) The teacher should announce the time for the second reading. The second reading time should be shorter than the first to encourage scanning for specific information.

9) Repeat Step 3.

10) Repeat Step 5, marking answers under Test 2. Students should not look at their first answers (Test 1) or at the article. (Answers on Test 2 may differ from those on Test 1.)

11) When the reading is particularly long or difficult, a third reading may be necessary. If so, the same procedures should be repeated. Students can fold their test papers to make a fresh surface for Test 3 answers.

12) After the last Comprehension Check, students can work together in small groups in checking their answers. Answers should be documented by reference to specific page and paragraph numbers in the article. The emphasis should be on *supporting* the answers. The teacher should encourage well-reasoned interpretations even if they disagree with the given answers.

The Comprehension Check should NEVER be used as a graded quiz. It is the student's personal record of progress and comprehension.

In order to teach another useful reading skill—initial surveying before a second, careful reading—we recommend that Steps 2 and 8 occasionally be reversed. When this is done, the reasons for change in procedure should first be explained to the students to avoid confusion and frustration.

In the beginning, students may show little improvement from Test 1 to Test 2 and, in some cases, scores may even drop. It is particularly important to remind students that it takes time and practice to develop reading skills— just as it does to develop any other skill. They should be encouraged to read the article again outside class for additional practice. With practice over a period of time, scores and comprehension should improve noticeably.

When the article is discussed in class, attention should generally be directed to sentence and paragraph content rather than to individual words. If a key word is unfamiliar, the students should be encouraged to guess the meaning from the context, and they should also be encouraged to see that words can have different meanings in different contexts.

Depending upon the students' needs and ability, there are several ways to review the article orally:

1)   The teacher can ask questions about the content.
2)   Students can ask each other questions about the content of specific paragraphs.
3)   Individual students can explain the meaning of a paragraph in their own words.
4)   Students can summarize the article orally as a class exercise.
5)   Students can bring related articles to class and give reports on them.

Reading-Skills Development—Exercises

The exercises in *Expanding Reading Skills: Intermediate* concentrate on three areas of reading skills development: 1) vocabulary development; 2) structural analysis; 3) relational and inferential analysis.

Both the *Analysis of Ideas* (Exercise A) and *Interpretation of Words and Phrases* (Exercise B) develop the student's ability to understand the inner meaning and to discover what is written "between the lines." In these exercises, many types of questions commonly used in schools in English-speaking countries have been included.

Analysis of Ideas and Relationships: This exercise will help the student develop the ability to distinguish between main and supporting ideas, to detect implications, interpret facts, and reach conclusions about the major points in the article. In this way, the student can develop skill in active, critical reading.

Interpretation of Words and Phrases: Important (and difficult) sentences, idioms, and concepts are singled out for analysis of meaning. This will lead to better understanding of the article.

Reading Reconstruction: This exercise provides the opportunity to practice some of the newly learned vocabulary in a short, clearly constructed paragraph. After reading the paragraph several times, the student can then try to restate the content of the paragraph (either orally or in writing). Another variation on this exercise is to read the paragraph to the students several times and then ask the students to reconstruct the content based upon their aural comprehension of the paragraph. We have used personal narrative as well as expository models in these paragraphs.

Antonyms: Vocabulary is extended through a study of word contrasts in a meaningful context.

Synonyms: Vocabulary is extended through a study of word similarities in a meaningful context.

Word Forms: Vocabulary is developed through a study of word families.

Vocabulary Application and Supplementary Vocabulary both provide the student with opportunities to practice newly learned vocabulary in a meaningful context.

Determiners and *Prepositions* concentrate on particular areas of language difficulty while using content from the article.

Sentence Scramble draws attention to the importance of word order in English. Words are presented in random order, and students are asked to make a meaningful sentence out of these words.

Cloze: In order to build an awareness of syntactic and semantic cues in language and, specifically, in print, the reader is asked to fill in blanks in a passage with *any* appropriate word. For the purpose of this exercise, it is not necessary or important for the student to supply the exact word found in the text. Any appropriate filler satisfying the semantic and syntactic constraints should be accepted.

Punctuation: To highlight common punctuation patterns (and options), students are asked to restore capital letters, commas, and periods to a paragraph.

Review Examinations

A short review examination appears after every four chapters.

1

TRIBALISM IS IMPORTANT IN AFRICA

[In Africa, everyone considers it important to be loyal to his own tribal group. This can be good for each person, but it can cause problems too. This article discusses some of the advantages and disadvantages of tribalism.]

1   A university student in Nairobi, Kenya, was stopped for a traffic violation the other day. The policeman took out his ticket book and asked, "What tribe are you?" In Lusaka, Zambia, a young man applying for a job was told to see the manager. He leaned over the receptionist's desk and asked, "What tribe is he?" When the receptionist told him that the manager was a Mashona, the applicant replied, "Then I'll never get the job."

2   This phenomenon is called tribalism. There are more than 2,000 tribes in black Africa. Each has its own language, customs, names, and physical characteristics that make its members almost immediately recognizable to a person from another tribe. To the Westerner, tribalism is one of the most difficult of African customs to understand. It makes many people think of savagery, warfare, or old-fashioned customs.

3   However, to most Africans, tribalism simply means very strong loyalty to one's ethnic group. It is a force that can be both good and bad. By definition tribalism means sharing among members of the extended family. It makes sure that a person is taken care of by his own group. To give a job to a fellow tribesman is not wrong; it is an obligation. Similarly, for a politician or military leader, it is considered good common sense to choose his closest advisers from

people of his own tribe. This ensures security, continuity, authority. Tribal loyalty may mean a quick promotion—from sergeant to captain, from clerk to manager—within a very short time.

4   Modern African politicians publicly speak out against tribal divisions. Yet it remains perhaps the most powerful force in day-to-day African life. As evidence of tribalism, in 1977 in Kenya, President Jomo Kenyatta's Kikuyu tribe controlled business and politics. Eight of the 21 cabinet posts, including the most important four, were filled by Kikuyus. In Uganda in the same year, the President's small Kakwa tribe filled almost all the highest government and military positions. In Angola, Ethiopia, and Nigeria, the fighting in the past ten years can be partly explained by disagreements among tribes.

5   One country that has largely avoided tribal problems is Tanzania. Some observers say this is partly because Tanzania has so many tribes (about 120) that none has been able to become a major force.

TURN TO COMPREHENSION CHECK AT END OF CHAPTER

READING TIMES:
1st reading _____ minutes
2nd reading _____ minutes

READING SPEED:
5 minutes = 76 wpm
4 minutes = 95 wpm
3 minutes = 127 wpm
2 minutes = 191 wpm

A. Analysis of Ideas and Relationships: Circle the letter next to the best answer.

1. In paragraph 1, why did the student reply "Then I'll never get the job?"
   a. Because he was a Mashona.
   b. Because he was not a Mashona.
   c. Because he couldn't do the job.

2. The two situations in paragraph 1 are examples of:
   a. typical young men in Africa.
   b. unusual problems.
   c. the importance of tribalism.

3. In paragraph 2, "Each has its own customs," **its** refers to:
   a. black Africa.
   b. tribe.
   c. members.

4. In paragraph 2, "It makes people think of old-fashioned customs," **it** refers to:
   a. tribalism.
   b. Westerner.
   c. difficult.

5. According to paragraph 3, what is the definition of tribalism?
   a. Giving a job to a fellow tribesman.
   b. A force that can be both good and bad.
   c. Sharing among members of the extended family.

6. In paragraph 3, one example of how a tribe takes care of its own people is:
   a. "tribal loyalty may mean a quick promotion."
   b. "very strong loyalty to one's ethnic group."
   c. "a force that can be both good and bad."

7. Find two more examples in paragraph 3 of how a person is taken care of by his own tribe:
   a. _____
   b. _____

8. In paragraph 4, "the most important four" refers to:
   a. cabinet posts.
   b. businesses.
   c. Kikuyus.

9. In paragraph 4, how many examples are there "as evidence of tribalism"? What are they?
   a. Three.
   b. Two.
   c. One.

10. In paragraph 5, **(about 120)** is in parentheses to show:
    a. that it is unimportant.
    b. how many tribes there are.
    c. that it is a large number.

B. Interpretation of Words and Phrases: Circle the letter next to the best answer.

1. A student was stopped for **a traffic violation.**
   a. stopping traffic
   b. breaking a traffic law
   c. walking into the traffic

2. The policeman **took out** his ticket book.
   a. put away
   b. tore up
   c. brought out

3. Tribalism means loyalty to the **ethnic group.**
   a. Africans
   b. political group that is in control
   c. people of one race or origin

4. Tribalism means sharing among members of the extended family. An **extended family** includes:
   a. parents, children, aunts, uncles, cousins, grandparents.
   b. parents and children only.
   c. sisters and brothers only.

5. It **makes sure** that a person is taken care of.
   a. guarantees
   b. forces
   c. hopes

6. It makes sure that a person is **taken care of.**
   a. stopped
   b. supported
   c. removed

7. It is **common sense** to choose advisers from his own group.
   a. sensible
   b. foolish
   c. ordinary

8. Modern politicians **speak out against** tribal divisions.
   a. shout loudly about
   b. agree with
   c. say that they are against

9. The fighting **in the past 10 years** can be partly explained by disagreements.
   a. 10 years ago
   b. from 10 years ago until now
   c. earlier than 10 years ago

10. Tanzania has **largely** avoided tribal problems.
    a. because of its large area
    b. never
    c. mainly

C. **Synonyms: From this list, choose a synonym for the word in bold type in each sentence.**

an advancement to a better job	faithful	power
answer	features	proof
bend	identifiable	safety
a duty		

1. Can you **lean** down and touch your toes?

2. I would appreciate your **reply** by next week.

3. This stew has the **characteristics** of Spanish cooking.

4. Mr. Pildar is easily **recognizable** by his bald head.

5. John has always remained **loyal** to his family and friends.

6. The fingerprints on the window were **evidence** of the crime.

7. For your own **security,** be sure to lock the door.

8. Who has the **authority** to sign this application?

9. Parents have **an obligation** to take care of their children.

10. Mrs. Luy received a **promotion** as assistant manager of the accounting department.

D. **Prepositions and Verb-Completers: Write any appropriate preposition or verb-completer in the blank spaces.**

1. The policeman took _____ his ticket book.

2. A young man applying _____ a job was told _____ see the manager.

3. Tribalism is one _____ the most difficult _____ African customs _____ understand.

4. It makes many people think _____ warfare.

5. _____ definition, tribalism means sharing _____ the members _____ one's own group.

6. He is taken care _____ _____ his own group.

7. It is considered common sense _____ choose advisers _____ his own tribe.

8. Tribal loyalty may mean a quick promotion _____ clerk _____ manager.

9. Tribalism is the most powerful force _____ day- _____ - day African life.

10. Eight _____ the posts were filled _____ Kikuyus.

E. **Determiners: Write any appropriate determiner in the blanks below. If no determiner is necessary, write an *"X"* in the blank.**

_____ university student in _____ Nairobi,
(1)   (2)
_____ Kenya, was stopped for _____ traffic violation
(3)   (4)
_____ other day. _____ policeman took out _____
(5)   (6)   (7)
ticket book and asked, " _____ what tribe are you?" In _____
(8)   (9)
Lusaka, _____ young man applying for _____ job was
(10)   (11)
told to see _____ manager. He leaned over _____ recep-
(12)   (13)
tionist's desk and asked, " _____ what tribe is he?" When
(14)
_____ receptionist told _____ him that _____
(15)   (16)   (17)
manager was _____ Mashona, _____ applicant replied,
(18)   (19)
"Then I'll never get _____ job."
(20)

F. Antonyms: Each sentence contains two opposite words. Circle the word that completes the sentence correctly.

1. Good citizens (violate–obey) the laws.

2. When the clerk added up my bill, I (took out–put away) my money.

3. Beads and shells are (old-fashioned–modern) forms of money.

4. I have finished all the exercises. I am (completely–partly) done.

5. It is (common sense–foolish) to see a doctor when you are very sick.

6. A (public–private) museum is open to everyone.

7. Shakespeare is a (major–minor) English writer.

8. If the people are (divided–united), they can make progress.

9. The United Nations (speaks out against–advocates) peace among nations.

10. The (leader–follower) walked in front of the group.

G. Word Forms: Choose the correct word form to fit into each sentence. Use appropriate verb tenses, singular or plural forms for nouns, and passive voice where necessary.

1. **manager, management, to manage, manageable**
   a. My teacher gives a _____ amount of homework.
   b. I can _____ to do all my homework in two hours.
   c. Mrs. Kuyper is the _____ of the office.
   d. Do you have the _____ skills to supervise a large office?

2. **thought, to think, thoughtful, thoughtfully**
   a. How _____ of you to remember my birthday!
   b. Everyone loves Jack because he acts so _____ .
   c. I have many _____ about my future.
   d. I _____ I'll visit my grandmother next Saturday.

3. **force, to force, forceful, forcefully**
   a. The angry man spoke very _____ .
   b. My parents _____ me to study hard when I was a child.
   c. People with a _____ personality usually get what they want.
   d. The car hit the house with such _____ that it broke the wall.

4. **sense, to sense, sensible, sensibly**
   a. It makes good _____ to bring an umbrella today; it's going to rain.
   b. Mrs. Vargas acted _____ and brought her umbrella.
   c. She did the _____ thing.
   d. It's so cloudy that I _____ it's going to rain.

5. **closeness, to close, close, closely**
   a. The child sat _____ to her mother.
   b. There is a special _____ between parents and children.
   c. _____ the box after you use it.
   d. He listened _____ while his advisers spoke.

6. **adviser, advice, to advise, advisable**
   a. I need some _____ with my problem.
   b. Speak to an _____ for help.
   c. He said it was _____ for me to go to college.
   d. My boss _____ me to study accounting.

7. **division, to divide, divisive**
   a. The Smiths _____ their time between work and school.
   b. _____ between the groups caused many problems.
   c. The two groups had many _____ problems.

8. **power, to power, powerful, powerfully**
   a. Gasoline _____ that engine.
   b. The policeman has the _____ to give you a ticket.
   c. The engine roared _____ .
   d. Is that medicine _____ or weak?

9. **evidence, evident, evidently**
   a. Do you have any _____ that Charles stole the money?
   b. It is _____ that no one is home. The lights are out.
   c. _____ , there is no one at home.

10. **part, to part, partly**
    a. Emilio _____ his hair on the left side.
    b. I like Florida _____ because of the weather.
    c. One _____ of the job is to answer the telephone.

H. Sentence Scramble: Make a sentence out of each group of words.

1. more – tribes – are – black – in – than – 2,000 – Africa – there

2. tribalism – of – among – the – means – sharing – members – family – extended

3. bad – is – a – can – good – and – it – that – both – force – be

4. may – quick – tribal – loyalty – promotion – a – mean

5. African – speak out – tribal – politicians – against – divisions

I.   Topics for Discussion and Composition:

1. In some countries, the family or the ethnic group is considered very important. There is great loyalty to this group and people feel very supportive of each other. In other countries, the individual person and his/her immediate family is the important group. Describe the pattern in your country. What is the important group? How does it function and help the members?

2. Think about your answer to question 1. Is the pattern of family groups in your native country similar to or different from African tribal groups? Please describe the similarities or differences between the family structure in your native country and in Africa.

3. In Africa, people live in extended families where parents, grandparents, children, aunts, uncles, and cousins stay close together and help each other. What are some of the advantages to this type of arrangement? What are some of the disadvantages?

4. Among African tribal groups, it is considered an obligation to give a job to a family member or tribe member. Do you agree that this is a good idea? What are the good points of giving a job to a family member? What are the bad points?

J. Reading Reconstruction: Read this paragraph as many times as you can in three minutes. Then, with your book closed, restate the ideas in writing as clearly and as completely as you can. Your teacher will write key words on the chalkboard. You do not have to use all of these words. They are offered only to help you remember. The emphasis in Reading Reconstruction is on comprehension and restatement of *ideas*. Make sure that your sentences are meaningful and that your grammatical structure is correct. (Note: If you wish to practice this type of exercise outside class you can do so easily by using short paragraphs taken from newspapers or magazines, following the above instructions.)

Cameroon, West Africa

Cameroon in West Africa is a nation of 24 separate languages and 200 tribal groups. The nation is also divided by three religions which compete for the loyalty of the 8 million people. However, Cameroon has managed to avoid problems with these ethnic and religious groups. This is partly due to its powerful president who has led the nation with authority for many years. In the past 10 years, Cameroon has also developed a strong economy. Rubber, coffee, bananas, and cotton are among the major products that give economic security to the country.

Key words (to be written on the chalkboard):

tribal	managed	powerful
groups	avoid	authority
divided	ethnic	major
loyalty	partly	security

K. Comprehension Check: On a separate piece of paper, write the numbers 1 through 10 on both sides. Mark one side "Test 1" and the other side "Test 2." Read each statement and decide whether it is true or false. Write "T" after true statements and "F" after false statements under Test 1. After you have finished the comprehension check, turn Test 1 face down. Then read the article again and do the comprehension check again under Test 2. Base your answers on the information in this article *only*, even if you disagree with what the author said.

1. There are more than 2,000 tribes in Africa.

2. Most tribes are very similar to each other.

3. To most Africans, tribalism means strong loyalty to one's group.

4. It is considered sensible to help people from a different tribe.

5. A person is usually taken care of by his own tribe.

6. Africans consider it an obligation to give a job to a fellow tribesman.

7. Modern African politicians approve of tribal divisions.

8. Tribalism is still a powerful force in day-to-day African life.

9. Much of the fighting in Africa recently has been due to tribal divisions.

10. Tanzania has serious tribal problems.

2

THE EARTH'S SPREADING DESERTS

[More than one-third of the earth's land is desert—very hot, dry, and difficult to live in. Today. the earth's deserts are spreading and getting larger. In some countries, the farm land along the edges of the desert is turning into desert too. Why is this happening? What can be done to save productive land?]

1   Only a generation ago, Mauritania's capital city was many days' walk from the Sahara. Today it is *in* the Sahara. The sand blows through the city streets and piles up against walls and fences. The desert stretches out as far as the eye can see.

2   In some parts of the Amazon rain forest in Brazil, all the trees have been cut down. The earth lies bare and dry in the hot sun. Nothing grows there anymore.

3   Over vast areas of every continent, the rainfall and **vegetation** necessary for life are disappearing. Already more than 40 percent of the earth's land is desert or desert-like. About 628 million people—one out of seven— live in these dry regions. In the past, they have managed to survive, but with difficulty. Now, largely through problems caused by modern life, their existence is threatened by the slow, steady spread of the earth's deserts.

plants

4   Many countries first became concerned in the 1970s after a terrible **drought** and **famine** destroyed Africa's Sahel, the fragile desert along the south edge of the Sahara. Thousands of people died even though there was a worldwide effort to send food and medicine to the starving people.

lack of water/ lack of food

5   Droughts and crop failures are not new in desert regions. They have been a fact of life for thousands of years. However, few people lived in desert regions in the past. They kept few animals, and they moved frequently. Today's problems are caused in great part by distinctly modern factors. In the Sahel, for example, Africans benefited from improvements in public health and modern farming methods. New water wells encouraged people to settle down on the land near the wells. The population grew. Farmers planted more crops and enlarged their **herds** of cattle, sheep, and goats. They became dependent on the new wells. When the drought came, the crops failed and the cattle ate all the grass around the overworked wells. The fragile land quickly lost its topsoil and became nothing but sand and dust.

groups

6   Many countries are experiencing similar problems. Poor land is farmed until it is worn out, and trees are cut for firewood, leaving the soil unprotected against wind and rain. In Peru, Chile, and Brazil, some areas that once were covered with forests now look like the moon. In India, some land has been so badly damaged by farming and tree cutting that **mud** now slides into the Indus and Ganges rivers. Cattle, sheep, and goats add to the problem by eating grass and other plants faster than they can grow back. In the United States, some highly populated areas (such as Los Angeles) are really deserts. Water must be **piped in** from hundreds of miles away—and this affects the water supply of other California communities.

wet soil

carried
through pipes

7   Scientists still do not understand all the complex problems of the desert, but there have been many ideas for saving the land. Saudi Arabia has planted 10 million trees to help keep the sand from taking over fertile areas. The Israelis are again using some of the water collection systems left by the ancient peoples in the Negev desert. They plan to water their orchards with the extra water. Some Sahel farmers still raise cattle on their poor farm land, but before the cattle are sold, they are taken to greener lands in the south to get fat.

8   The spread of the deserts affects most countries. The big question today is, how can an expanding world population find food and space without destroying the land it lives on? For many countries, battling the desert is the only chance to avoid starvation, destruction, and disaster.

TURN TO COMPREHENSION CHECK AT END OF CHAPTER

READING TIMES:
1st reading _____ minutes
2nd reading _____ minutes

READING SPEED:
6 minutes = 100 wpm
5 minutes = 120 wpm
4 minutes = 150 wpm
3 minutes = 200 wpm
2 minutes = 300 wpm

A. **Analysis of Ideas and Relationships: Circle the letter next to the best answer.**

1. According to paragraph 1, what has happened in Mauritania?
   a. It takes many days to walk through the Sahara.
   b. Mauritania has moved its capital city into the Sahara.
   c. The Sahara has spread until it reached Mauritania's capital.

2. In paragraph 3, "one out of seven" refers to:
   a. the number of people who live in dry regions.
   b. the percentage of the earth's land that is desert-like.
   c. more than a third of the land's earth.

3. In paragraph 4, what is the **Sahel**?
   a. The great drought and famine in Africa.
   b. The desert along the south edge of the Sahara.
   c. The death of thousands of people.

4. In paragraph 5, improvements in public health and modern farming methods are examples of:
   a. distinctly modern factors.
   b. the droughts and crop failures.
   c. a fact of life in dry regions.

5. In paragraph 5, "The land became nothing but sand and dust" describes:
   a. the success of modern factors.
   b. what the topsoil looks like.
   c. the result of a severe drought.

6. In paragraph 6, "many countries are experiencing similar problems." **Similar** refers to:
   a. simple problems.
   b. the problems discussed in paragraph 5.
   c. problems that have existed for thousands of years.

7. Paragraph 6 says "trees are cut for firewood." This is an example of:
   a. Peru's problems.
   b. India's problems.
   c. both a and b.

8. In paragraph 7, "they are taken to the greener lands in the south." **They** refers to:
   a. the Sahel farm land.
   b. the farmers.
   c. the cattle.

9. In paragraph 7, how many ideas for saving the land are described?
   a. Three.
   b. Four.
   c. Five.
   What are they?

10. In paragraph 8, the words "starvation, destruction, and disaster":
    a. have no emotional meaning.
    b. are used because a group of nouns is considered good style at the end of an article.
    c. are emotional words used to emphasize the terrible situation.

B. Interpretation of Words and Phrases: Circle the letter next to the best answer.

1. Only a generation ago, Mauritania's capital was far from the desert. In this sentence, **generation** means:
   a. creation of living things.
   b. production of electricity.
   c. the number of years between an adult and a child.

2. Thousands of people died even though there was a worldwide effort to send food. **Worldwide** means:
   a. everywhere in the world.
   b. as big as the world.
   c. country by country.

3. Crop failures have been **a fact of life** for thousands of years.
   a. unimportant to the people's lives
   b. a rare occurrence that surprises people
   c. a regular part of life that can't be changed

4. Today's problems are caused **in great part** by modern factors.
   a. slightly
   b. mostly
   c. quickly

5. New water wells encouraged people to **settle down** near the wells.
   a. stay in one place
   b. walk around
   c. grow crops

6. The cattle ate all the grass around the overworked wells. **Overworked** means:
   a. dug very deep in the ground.
   b. in excellent condition.
   c. used too much.

7. Poor land is farmed until it **is worn out**.
   a. becomes useless
   b. is thrown away
   c. is fertilized again

8. The areas now **look like the moon**.
   a. look as bright as the moon at night
   b. resemble the moon's empty surface
   c. seem as far away as the moon

9. Saudi Arabia has planted 10 million trees to **keep** the sand from taking over fertile areas.
   a. watch
   b. prevent
   c. increase

10. Saudi Arabia has planted the trees to keep the sand from **taking over** fertile areas.
    a. leaving
    b. gaining control over
    c. watering

C. Synonyms: From this list, choose a synonym for the word in bold type in each sentence.

border	elements	motivated
clearly	expanded	opportunity
constant	gathering	very large
delicate		

1. The encyclopedia contains a **vast** number of subjects.

2. It is better to drive your car at a **steady** rate than to stop and start a lot.

3. The use of English as the international business language has **spread** all over the world.

4. These dishes are quite **fragile**. Be careful with them!

5. The Shimadas built a fence around the **edge** of their property.

6. I **distinctly** remember meeting you at Steve's party last year.

7. What are the major **factors** of the problem in the desert?

8. The teacher **encouraged** her students to study hard.

9. The water **collection** system in the Negev was built many years ago.

10. Did you have the **chance** to see Hollywood when you went to California?

D. Prepositions and Verb-Completers: Write any appropriate prepositions or verb-completer in the blank spaces.

1. The sand blows _____ the city streets and piles _____ _____ walls and fences.

2. One _____ _____ seven people lives _____ dry regions.

3. They have managed _____ live there but _____ difficulty.

4. Their existence is threatened _____ the slow spread _____ the deserts.

5. The Sahel is the desert _____ the south edge _____ the Sahara.

6. They became dependent _____ the new wells.

7. Trees are cut _____ firewood, leaving the soil unprotected _____ wind and rain.

8. The cattle ate all the grass _____ the wells.

9. _____ India, mud now slides _____ the Indus and Ganges rivers.

10. Saudi Arabia has planted 10 million trees _____ keep the sand _____ taking _____ fertile areas.

E. Determiners: Write any appropriate determiner in the blanks below. If no determiner is necessary, write an "X" in the blank.

More than _____ 40 percent of _____ earth's land is
(1)   (2)
desert or _____ desert-like. One out of _____ seven people
(3)   (4)
lives in _____ dry regions. In _____ past, they have
(5)   (6)
managed to survive. Now _____ existence is threatened by
(7)
_____ slow spread of _____ deserts. _____ many
(8)   (9)   (10)
countries first became concerned in _____ 1970s after
(11)
_____ terrible drought destroyed _____ Africa's Sahel,
(12)   (13)
_____ desert along _____ south edge of _____
(14)   (15)   (16)
Sahara. _____ thousands of _____ people died even
(17)   (18)
though there was _____ worldwide effort to send _____
(19)   (20)
food and medicine.

F. Supplementary Vocabulary: Use each phrase in an original sentence.

1. only a generation ago
2. more than _____ percent of
3. in the past
4. largely through problems caused by
5. a worldwide effort (to, before, after, when)
6. has been a fact of life
7. when the (drought, storm, snow, monsoon) came
8. adds to the problem by
9. there have been many ideas for

G. **Word Forms: Choose the correct word form to fit into each sentence. Use appropriate verb tenses, singular or plural forms for nouns, and passive voice where necessary.**

1. **dryness, to dry, dry, dried**
   a. The _____ of the soil ruined the crops.
   b. My throat is so _____ . I need a drink of water.
   c. I like to eat _____ fruit as a snack.
   d. After you _____ the dishes, please put them in the closet.

2. **to enlarge, large, largely**
   a. Their problems are due _____ to poor planning.
   b. Bryce's Department Store _____ its furniture department about a year ago.
   c. I'm looking for a _____ desk.

3. **failure, to fail, failing**
   a. My grandfather is in _____ health and can't hear much any more.
   b. I have never _____ a test. How about you?
   c. His _____ to pay taxes on time caused him lots of trouble.

4. **distinction, to distinguish, distinct, distinctive, distinctly, distinctively**
   a. Mrs. Karnowsky has the _____ of being the oldest person to graduate from this college.
   b. I _____ remember the events that led up to the accident.
   c. John's girlfriend always wears _____ jewelry.
   d. She also dresses very _____ .
   e. The words on that page aren't very _____ . I can hardly read them.
   f. Can you _____ different wines from each other by their taste?

5. **population, to populate, populated**
   a. Which is the most heavily _____ city in the world?
   b. Some countries are trying to re-_____ the desert areas by developing new methods to save the land.
   c. Year by year, the _____ in the desert areas is becoming poorer.

6. **dependent, to depend, dependent**
   a. My wife and two children are my _____ .
   b. Children are _____ on their parents for many years.
   c. Don't _____ on Freddie to buy the tickets; he always forgets!

7. **poverty, poor, poorly**
   a. How many people in the world live in _____ ?
   b. Farmers can't produce much food on _____ land.
   c. I did very _____ the first time I took my driver's test.

8. **protection, to protect, protected, protective, protectively**
   a. The princess lived a _____ life.
   b. If you are too _____ of your children, they will never learn to deal with life's difficulties.
   c. My health insurance _____ me if I get sick.
   d. Trees are a good _____ against soil loss.
   e. The mother bear stood _____ in front of her baby cubs.

9. **addition, to add, additional, additionally**
   a. Every month, Mrs. Kelly _____ up all her bills before she pays them.
   b. In _____ to my parents, my two brothers live with me.
   c. Besides the lack of rain, there are _____ reasons why the deserts are spreading.
   d. I don't have enough money to buy a car. _____ , I don't have a place to park one.

10. **planner, plan, to plan, planned**
    a. I have a _____ that will make me a millionaire!
    b. The city _____ suggested that more parks should be built.
    c. When Alberto finishes school, he _____ to join a computer company.
    d. An organized person does everything in a _____ way.

H. Sentence Scramble: Make a sentence out of each group of words.

1. sand – streets – the – the – blows – city – through

2. distinctly – factors – today's – are – modern – by – problems – caused – in great part

3. failed – when – crops – drought – came – the – the

4. in – some – really – deserts – highly populated – United States – are – the – areas

5. saving – land – there – been – ideas – have – for – many – the

I. Topics for Discussion and Composition:

1. "The problems of the deserts today are caused by distinctly modern factors." This article discusses a complex problem: modern technology tries to make life better for the people in the deserts, but actually makes it worse. Do you think that modern technology is always the best answer to solve problems? Are there times when traditional ways are better? Please give several reasons and examples to explain your answer.

2. Do you know of some examples where modern technology benefited people? Please describe these situations.

3. Do you know of some examples where modern technology made a problem worse? Please describe.

4. Some areas that were not deserts in the past are becoming deserts now because too many people live in too small an area. They are over-farming the land and cutting down all the trees. Do you think the earth can support a constantly growing population? If yes, what will need to be done to provide food and living space? If no, what do you think will happen to the earth as the population continues to grow?

5. "Population control is the answer to the world's problems." Do you agree or disagree? Why? Please give several reasons for your answer and illustrate your reasons with specific examples.

J. Reading Reconstruction: Read this paragraph as many times as you can in three minutes. Then, with your book closed, try to restate the ideas as clearly and completely as you can. (See Chapter 1 for complete instructions.)

The Spreading Deserts

The spread of the desert is not new. In ancient times, for example, the Middle East was a very fertile area. For hundreds of years, desert peoples moved from place to place with their animals before an area was destroyed. This gave the land a chance to recover. They also raised crops every other year in an area, so they never overworked the land. These traditional ways are disappearing, largely because of modern technology. Today, many factors add to the problem along the edge of the desert. The population is growing, and too many animals feed on the fragile land. There is now a worldwide effort to stop the spread of the desert. This may be the last chance to save the land.

Key words (to be written on the chalkboard):

spread	overworked	population
ancient	largely	fragile
fertile	technology	worldwide
chance	factors	
raised	add	
crops	edge	

K. Comprehension Check: On a separate piece of paper, write the numbers 1 through 10 on both sides. Mark one side "Test 1" and the other side "Test 2." Read each statement and decide whether it is true or false. Write "T" after true statements and "F" after false statements under Test 1. After you have finished the comprehension check, turn Test 1 face down. Then read the article again and do the comprehension check again under Test 2. Base your answers on the information in this article *only*, even if you disagree with what the author said.

1. One out of 10 people lives in dry regions.

2. Their life in the desert is threatened now by traditional problems.

3. The earth's deserts are slowly spreading.

4. New water wells can solve the problems in Africa's deserts.

5. Many countries are experiencing problems that will cause their deserts to spread.

6. If too many trees are cut for firewood, more trees grow back and there is no problem.

7. Animals sometimes eat plants faster than the plants can grow back.

8. Scientists understand all the problems of the desert.

9. It is impossible to do battle against the spread of the desert.

10. There are many ideas for saving the desert.

3

LIVING A LONG LIFE

[The man in this picture is 102 years old. He leads a full, active life. Why has he lived so long? Many scientists would like to know the answer to this question. They are studying groups of people all over the world who live to very old ages. This article describes some of these groups of old people and how they live.]

1   In the Caucasus region of the Soviet Union, nearly 50 out of every 100,000 people live to celebrate their 100th birthday, and many don't stop at 100! By comparison, in America only 3 people in 100,000 reach 100. But these Soviet old people aren't alone. The Pakistani Hunzas, who live high in the Himalaya Mountains, and the Vilcabambans of the Andes Mountains in Ecuador seem to share the secret of long life too.

2   These peoples remain healthy in body and spirit despite the passage of time. While many older persons in industrial societies become weak and ill in their 60s and 70s, some Soviet Georgians, aged 110 to 140, work in the fields beside their great-great-grandchildren. Even the idea of aging is foreign to them. When asked, "At what age does youth end?" most of these old people had no answer. Several replied, "Well, perhaps at age 80." The very youngest estimate was age 60.

3   What accounts for this ability to survive to such old age, and to survive so well? First of all, hard physical work is a way of life for *all* of these long-lived peoples. They begin their long days of physical labor as children and never seem to stop. For example, Mr. Rustam Mamedov is 142 years of age. He remembers his life experiences: the Crimean War of 1854; the Turkish War of 1878; the Bolshevik Revolution in 1917. His wife is 116 years old. They have been married for 90

years. Mr. Mamedov has no intentions of retiring from his life as a farmer. "Why? What else would I do?" he asks. Oh, he's slowed down a bit. Now he might quit for the day after 6 hours in the field instead of 10.

4 All these people get healthful rewards from the environment in which they work. They all come from mountainous regions. They live and work at elevations of 5,000 to 12,000 feet (1,660 to 4,000 meters) above sea level. The air has less oxygen and is pollution-free. This reduced-oxygen environment makes the heart and blood vessel system stronger.

5 Another factor that may contribute to the good health of these people is their isolation. To a great extent, they are separated from the pressures and worries of industrial society.

6 Inherited factors also play some role. Most of the longest-lived peoples had parents and grandparents who also reached very old ages. Good family genes may, therefore, be one factor in living longer.

7 Finally, although these three groups don't eat exactly the same foods, their diets are similar. The Hunzas, Vilcabambans, and Soviets eat little animal meat. Their diets are full of fresh fruits, vegetables, nuts, grains, cheese, and milk. They never eat more food than their bodies need.

city 8 It is clear that isolation from **urban** pressures and pollution, clean mountain air, daily hard work, moderate diets, good genes, and a youthful approach to life all contribute to the health and remarkable long life of all these people.

TURN TO COMPREHENSION CHECK AT END OF CHAPTER

READING TIMES:
1st reading _____ minutes
2nd reading _____ minutes

READING SPEED:
6 minutes = 82 wpm
5 minutes = 98 wpm
4 minutes = 123 wpm
3 minutes = 164 wpm

A. Analysis of Ideas and Relationships: Circle the letter next to the best answer.

1. What is the main subject of this article?
   a. Mr. Mamedov's life.
   b. A description of several societies where people live a long time.
   c. Suggestions for how you can live a long life.

2. Paragraph 1:
   a. introduces the subject of this article.
   b. tells why Americans don't live as long as other people.
   c. tells you some secrets about the Hunzas.

3. On this chart, where are the **great-great-grandchildren**? Write the name of each generation.

1. _me_
2. _my children_
3. _____
4. _____
5. _____
6. _____

4. In paragraph 3, the description of Mr. Mamedov is:
   a. an example of a typical long life among these people.
   b. an example of an unusual long life among these people.
   c. an explanation of why he is still healthy.

5. Paragraph 4 describes:
   a. their isolation.
   b. inherited factors.
   c. the mountain environment.

6. Paragraph 5 describes:
   a. their isolation.
   b. inherited factors.
   c. the mountain environment.

7. Paragraph 6 describes:
   a. their isolation.
   b. inherited factors.
   c. the mountain environment.

8. The subject of paragraph 7 is:
   a. isolation.
   b. inherited factors.
   c. food and diet.

9. This article concludes that _____ contribute to the remarkable long life of these peoples.
   a. moderate diets
   b. clean mountain air
   c. daily hard work
   d. all the above factors

10. How do you think the author feels about these long-lived people? Why did you choose your answer?
    a. He is impressed with them.
    b. He doesn't care.
    c. He doesn't like them.

B.   Interpretation of Words and Phrases: Circle the letter next to the best answer.

1. 50 out of 100,000 people in the Caucasus live to celebrate their 100th birthday, and many **don't stop at 100.**
   a. travel more than 100 miles
   b. have more than 100 people in their family
   c. live longer than age 100

2. **By comparison**, only 3 Americans in 100,000 live until the age of 100.
   a. On the other hand,
   b. Also,
   c. Sadly,

3. The Hunzas and Vilcabambans **share the secret of** long life too.
   a. also know about
   b. won't tell anyone about
   c. wish they could explain about

4. These people remain healthy despite **the passage of time**.
   a. having time to do what they want
   b. being on time
   c. time going by

5. The idea of **aging** is foreign to them.
   a. growing old
   b. having a birthday
   c. knowing your age

6. Hard work is **a way of life** for all these people.
   a. a long road
   b. the usual condition of life
   c. not a regular part of the day's work

7. He **has slowed down**.
   a. moves more slowly
   b. runs downhill
   c. takes better care of himself

8. He has slowed down **a bit**.
   a. on purpose
   b. a lot
   c. a little

9. **To a great extent**, they are separated from the pressures of industrial society.
   a. For the most part,
   b. Truly,
   c. However,

10. Inherited factors **play some role in** their long life.
    a. contribute to
    b. act in
    c. have no meaning for

C. **Synonyms: From this list, choose a synonym for the word in bold type in each sentence.**

adds to	precisely
area	stop working because of old age
continue to live	stresses
guessed	surprising
medium	surroundings

1. Many people in this **region** live to be 100 years old.

2. He **estimated** that youth ended at age 80.

3. Many Hunzas **survive** to a very old age.

4. What will you do when you **retire**?

5. They live in very healthful **environments**.

6. Isolation **contributes to** their good health.

7. They don't have the **pressures** of industrial society.

8. They don't eat **exactly** the same foods.

9. They eat a **moderate** amount of food.

10. Moderate diets contribute to the **remarkable** long life of all these people.

D. **Prepositions and Verb-Completers: Write any appropriate preposition or verb-completer in the blank spaces.**

1. Nearly 50 out _____ every 100,000 people live _____ celebrate their 100th birthday.

2. _____ what age does youth end?

3. What accounts _____ this ability _____ survive _____ such old age?

4. First _____ all, hard work is a way _____ life.

5. He has been married _____ 90 years.

6. He has no intention _____ retiring _____ his life as a farmer.

7. He's slowed _____ a bit.

8. He might quit _____ the day _____ six hours _____ the field.

9. They get healthful rewards _____ their environment.

10. _____ a great extent, they are separated _____ the pressures _____ industrial society.

E. **Determiners: Write any appropriate determiner in the blanks below. If no determiner is necessary, write an "X" in the blank.**

_____ peoples remain healthy in _____ body and
_____(1)_____ spirit despite _____ passage of time. While _____ older
_____(3)_____ _____(4)_____
persons in _____ industrial societies become _____ weak
_____(5)_____ _____(6)_____
and ill in _____ 60s and 70s, _____ Soviet Georgians, aged
_____(7)_____ _____(8)_____
_____ 100 to _____ 140, work in _____ fields
_____(9)_____ _____(10)_____ _____(11)_____
beside _____ great-great-grandchildren. Even _____ idea
_____(12)_____ _____(13)_____
of _____ aging is _____ foreign to them. When asked, "At
_____(14)_____ _____(15)_____
_____ what age does youth _____ end?" _____
_____(16)_____ _____(17)_____ _____(18)_____
most of _____ old people had no _____ answer.
_____(19)_____ _____(20)_____

F. **Vocabulary Application: Read each situation. Then comment on it by using each word in an original sentence. You may use any verb tense or word form or change nouns from singular to plural.**

1. When Noah and Mary Barnett married on February 1, 1899, Mr. Barnett's mother didn't attend the ceremony. She didn't think the marriage would last. But 79 years later, the Barnetts, both 98, are still married and in love. They have lived in the same house for 71 years and have raised five children who have given them 151 grandchildren and great-grandchildren. Mr. Barnett says he has loved Mary since they were five. "She was the prettiest girl I ever saw, in her bright red shoes," he remembers. "Even now she is pretty. Not to you, maybe. But to me she is."

   celebrate:
   remarkable:
   reward:
   despite the passage of time:
   survive:
   to a great extent:

2. Women outlive men by an average of 8 years. A California study compared the life and health behaviors of men and women. They found that women actually had more unhealthy behaviors than men, but despite this, they lived longer. The highest risk factors for men included smoking, drinking, and not being married. For women they were smoking, physical inactivity, and few social contacts. There is some indication that hormones, not behaviors, influence the length of life for men and women.

   survive:
   similar:
   contribute:
   moderate:
   by comparison:
   play some role:

G. Word Forms: Choose the correct word form to fit into each sentence. Use appropriate verb tenses, singular or plural forms for nouns, and passive voice where necessary.

1. **region, regional, regionally**
   a. Mr. Dufy comes from a mountainous _____ of France.
   b. There are many _____ foods in my native country.
   c. Is the electric power system controlled _____ or nationally in your country?

2. **celebration, celebrity, to celebrate**
   a. I _____ my birthday on March 28.
   b. Our family had a big _____ when my brother got married.
   c. That man is a famous movie _____ .

3. **passage, passenger, to pass, past**
   a. After you _____ the department store, you'll arrive at the museum.
   b. You must walk through the underground _____ to get across that busy street.
   c. The car drove _____ me very quickly.
   d. There were so many _____ on the bus that I couldn't get a seat.

4. **industry, industrialization, industrialist, to industrialize, industrious, industrial, industrially**
   a. Many nations are planning to increase _____ to help their economy.
   b. They are trying to _____ themselves quickly.
   c. Many _____ products are exported to other countries.
   d. One of the most famous _____ in the United States was Henry Ford.
   e. The largest _____ in the United States are automobiles and steel.
   f. Japan is one of the most _____-advanced nations in the world.
   g. My _____ friend works all day and goes to school at night too.

5. **ability, to enable, able, ably**
   a. Pedro has the _____ to do great things with his life.
   b. His great intelligence will _____ him to get a scholarship to college.
   c. He is _____ to learn quickly.
   d. He did the job so _____ that everyone praised him.

6. **survivor, survival, to survive, surviving**
   a. That man is the only _____ of the car accident.
   b. His _____ was due to luck.
   c. It is difficult _____ in the desert.
   d. After the old woman's death, the _____ members of her family divided up her possessions.

7. **intention, to intend, intentional, intentionally**
   a. We _____ to get married next month.
   b. The bad child threw that rock at me _____ .
   c. Do you think his actions were _____ , or were they accidental?
   d. I have no _____ of climbing up that steep hill!

8. **reward, to reward, rewarding**
   a. Mr. and Mrs. Allen are offering a _____ for their lost dog.
   b. Should parents _____ their children when they are good?
   c. Getting a college degree was the most _____ experience of my life.

9. **worry, to worry, worrisome, worried**
   a. You look _____ . Is something wrong?
   b. These problems are very _____ . I don't know what to do.
   c. Mr. Santos always _____ a lot.
   d. My biggest _____ is getting good grades.

10. **similarity, similar, similarly**
    a. There is a great _____ between Spanish and Italian.
    b. _____ , Norwegian and Swedish are very much alike.
    c. These two languages have many _____ words.

H. Sentence Scramble: Make a sentence out of each group of words.

1. peoples – in – and – remain – healthy – these – body – spirit

2. does – at – end – age – what – youth

3. he – might – six – quit – after – hours

4. these – people – rewards – from – get – healthful – environment – their

5. fresh – are – full – their – fruits – diets – of

I. Topics for Discussion and Composition:

1. This article describes several groups of people who live to very old ages. Do any groups of people live to be unusually old in your native country? If so, describe them. If not, do you think there are specific reasons why people don't live so long? (Examples: diet, urban pressures, pollution, societal pressures, etc.)

2. The three groups of people described in this article remain active and appreciated in their societies all their lives. Are older persons in your native country treated this way too? What is their position in society? Are they important or unimportant, respected or disregarded, etc.? Do they contribute to the community, the family, the society? Please give some examples.

3. In some countries, older persons are considered unimportant and unwanted. They might live out their old age away from their children, possibly in nursing homes or hospitals. Does this happen in your native country? What is your opinion of this situation?

4. In this article, some Soviet Georgians said that youth ends "perhaps at age 80." When do you think youth ends? Why do you think so? How long will you remain youthful?

J. Reading Reconstruction: Read this paragraph as many times as you can in three minutes. Then, with your book closed, try to restate the ideas as clearly and completely as you can. (See Chapter 1 for complete instructions.)

He's 84—and Still Not Too Old for the Job

When Nathan Lippman was hired as an accountant, he replaced a 60-year-old man who retired from the job. Now, 52 years later, Lippman is 84 years old and still working as the treasurer of the company. He has survived the change over the years from using paper and pencil to using computers. "He is as active as when he began. He's remarkable," says the company president. Mr. Lippman says, "I find it rewarding to keep on working. I never worried about becoming the president of the company. I just like to contribute and do my job well." Sometimes he thinks about retirement, but he says he's not ready to slow down yet.

Key words (to be written on the chalkboard):

accountant	computers	contribute
retired	remarkable	retirement
treasurer	rewarding	slow down
survived	worried	

K. Comprehension Check: On a separate piece of paper, write the numbers 1 through 10 on both sides. Mark one side "Test 1" and the other side "Test 2." Read each statement and decide whether it is true or false. Write "T" after true statements and "F" after false statements under Test 1. After you have finished the comprehension check, turn Test 1 face down. Then read the article again and do the comprehension check again under Test 2. Base your answers on the information in this article *only,* even if you disagree with what the author said.

1. Only the Hunzas in the Himalayas live to very old ages.

2. Hard work is a way of life for all the long-lived peoples mentioned in this article.

3. They all live in mountainous regions.

4. They all think that youth ends at age 20.

5. The reduced-oxygen environment in the mountains is good for the heart.

6. These people seem to worry a lot.

7. The people who live a long time generally had parents and grandparents who lived a long time too.

8. These people eat a moderate amount of food.

9. These people eat a lot of meat.

10. Daily hard work and isolation from pressures contribute to their remarkable health and long life.

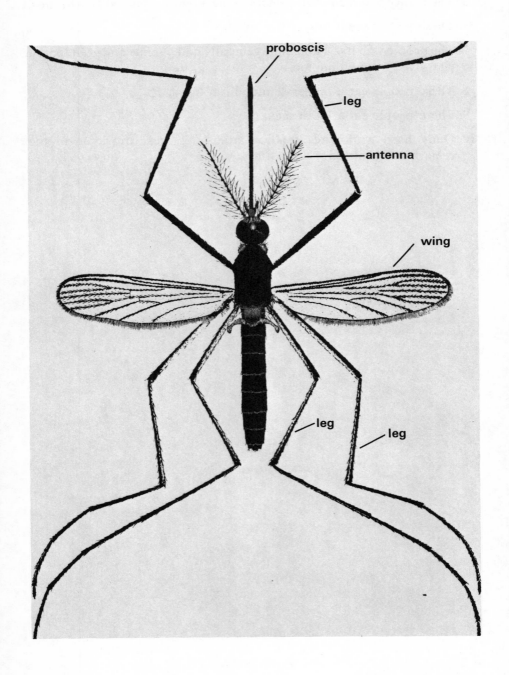

4

THE FEMALE MOSQUITO

[Everyone everywhere in the world knows the mosquito. The female of this insect bites people and animals because she needs blood to reproduce. Her bite usually leaves an itchy spot on your skin. This article tells you all about the female mosquito and how she lives.]

1   No matter who you are or where you come from, one thing is certain: you are acquainted with the mosquito—although you probably wish you weren't. Mosquitoes are everywhere. They can be found all over the world, and they come in more than 2,500 **species.** Somewhere, at some time, you have surely met at least one.

types

2   No one loves the mosquito. But unfortunately the mosquito may decide that she loves you. *She?* Yes, *she.* Did you know that only the female mosquito bites? Well, it's true. And it's not because she's unfriendly; she needs blood to reproduce.

3   Do you know how the female mosquito decides whom to bite? She's quite selective, and she chooses her victims carefully. First, she uses sensors to find her victim. These sensors are located on her two antennae and her three pairs of legs. With these sensors, she tests your body moisture, body warmth, and chemical substances in your sweat. If she likes what she finds, she bites. But if you don't appeal to her, she'll reject you for someone more **appetizing.** The next time a mosquito bites you, just remember that you were chosen. You're special.

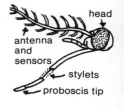

better tasting

4   If the mosquito likes you, she **settles** onto your flesh very gently, and she breaks your skin with her proboscis tip. Proboscis tip? What's *that*? It's a kind of mouth and it sticks out just below the mosquito's eyes.

lands

43

It contains six sharp instruments called stylets. She stabs all six stylets into your skin at once, and if she hits a blood vessel, she'll get a full dinner in about a minute. All this usually takes place so quickly and quietly that you may not have suspected anything was happening.

liquid in the mouth/becoming solid

5   Why does a mosquito bite itch? The itch is not really from the bite. It's from the **saliva** the mosquito mixes with your blood to keep it from **clotting** as she sucks it up her proboscis tip. By the time the itching begins, she has gone.

6   And then what happens? Well, after her delicious dinner, the mosquito is tired. She just wants to find a place to rest. Heavy with your blood, she picks a spot—on a leaf or a wall or a stone—to quietly lay her eggs. Just one drop of blood will produce hundreds of eggs.

sex partner

7   Where is her **mate**? Well, their relationship is over, and he's no longer around. Their mating took place before she bit you. She will live one to two months and lay eggs four or five times during this time.

8   All mosquitoes, male and female, pass through their early stages of development in or near water. In fact, mosquito eggs will not hatch without water—although the eggs can survive up to five years on dry land waiting for water. It is not surprising that heavy rains produce large numbers of mosquitoes.

take the time
irritate

9   But why? Why did nature **bother** to create mosquitoes? Just to **annoy** us? Probably that wasn't the main reason. Male mosquitoes live on the nectar of flowers, and some scientists believe that they pollinate the flowers as they fly from one to the other. Of course, mosquitoes have to reproduce, and unfortunately that's where you and I come in. Like it or not, mosquitoes are here to stay. Ouch! (Slap!) One just bit me!

TURN TO COMPREHENSION CHECK AT END OF CHAPTER

READING TIMES:
1st reading _____ minutes
2nd reading _____ minutes

READING SPEED:
6 minutes = 91 wpm
5 minutes = 109 wpm
4 minutes = 137 wpm
3 minutes = 182 wpm

A. Analysis of Ideas and Relationships: Circle the letter next to the best answer.

1. In paragraph 1, "you have surely met at least one," **one** refers to:
   a. mosquito.
   b. somewhere.
   c. person.

2. In paragraph 2, "no one loves the mosquito," **one** refers to:
   a. mosquito.
   b. somewhere.
   c. person.

3. In paragraph 2, why is "*she?*" written in italics?
   a. For emphasis.
   b. Because it is a short question.
   c. For no special reason.

4. According to paragraph 4, what is a proboscis tip?
   a. The mosquito's eyes.
   b. A kind of mouth.
   c. Both a and b.

5. According to paragraph 5, when does the itching begin?
   a. As the mosquito sucks up your blood.
   b. While the mosquito is biting you.
   c. After the mosquito leaves.

6. According to paragraph 6, what did she eat for her delicious dinner?
   a. Your blood.
   b. A leaf.
   c. I don't know.

7. According to paragraph 7, where is her mate?
   a. He died.
   b. He went away.
   c. He's still with her.

8. Paragraph 9 says "unfortunately that's where you and I come in." Why is it unfortunate?
   a. Because mosquitoes have to reproduce.
   b. Because mosquitoes will bite us to get some blood.
   c. Because mosquitoes are here to stay.

9. According to paragraph 9, "Ouch! (Slap!)." What happened?
   a. A mosquito bit the writer, and the writer hit her.
   b. A mosquito slapped the writer and flew away.
   c. A mosquito flew away, and the writer hit himself.

10. There are many words associated with pain in this article. Match the synonyms.
    a. break   1. pierce
    b. slap   2. drink in
    c. stab   3. cut with your teeth
    d. bite   4. bother
    e. suck   5. hit
    f. annoy   6. crack

B. Interpretation of Words and Phrases: Circle the letter next to the best answer.

1. **No matter** who you are, you are acquainted with the mosquito.
   a. especially
   b. it is very important
   c. regardless of

2. **It sticks out** just below the mosquito's eyes.
   a. hurts
   b. protrudes
   c. rests

3. She stabs all six stylets into your skin **at once.**
   a. at the same time
   b. one at a time
   c. only one time

4. She'll get a full dinner **in about a minute.**
   a. in approximately a minute
   b. in less than a minute
   c. in five minutes

5. All this usually **takes place** very quickly and quietly.
   a. is located
   b. happens
   c. eats

6. In paragraph 6, **heavy with your blood** means:
   a. your blood is heavy.
   b. the mosquito is heavy.
   c. the mosquito is tired.

7. "Just one drop of blood will produce hundreds of eggs." In this sentence, **drop** means:
   a. falling
   b. drink.
   c. very small amount.

8. He's **no longer** around.
   a. not . . . anymore
   b. still
   c. short

9. **It is not surprising** that heavy rains produce many mosquitoes.
   a. I am very surprised
   b. I am not surprised
   c. I never knew

10. **Like it or not,** mosquitoes are here to stay.
    a. It doesn't matter whether mosquitoes like the situation or not.
    b. It doesn't matter if we get bitten by mosquitoes.
    c. It doesn't matter whether we like the situation or not.

C. **Synonyms: From this list, choose a synonym for the word in bold type in each sentence.**

chooses	particular	skin irritation
guessed	point	sure
interests	sets of two	tool
multiply		

1. I am **certain** that I left my hat in the restaurant.

2. Mosquitoes need blood in order to **reproduce.**

3. Be very **selective** when you choose a mate.

4. Gloves, glasses, and twins come in **pairs.**

5. The thought of a good dinner followed by a relaxing evening **appeals to** me very much.

6. You can't write if the **tip** of your pencil is broken.

7. What kind of **instrument** did the mechanic use to fix the engine?

8. Felipe **suspected** that his friends were making a surprise party for him, but he pretended that he didn't know.

9. If you touch poison ivy, you will get a terrible **itch.**

10. Janie always **picks** good movies. You can trust her judgment.

D. Prepositions and Verb-Completers: Write any appropriate preposition or verb-completer in the blank spaces.

1. You are acquainted _____ the mosquito.

2. Mosquitoes need blood _____ reproduce.

3. These sensors are located _____ her two antennae and _____ her three pairs _____ legs.

4. If you don't appeal _____ her, she'll reject you _____ someone more appetizing.

5. The proboscis tip sticks _____ just _____ the mosquito's eyes.

6. She stabs all six stylets _____ your skin _____ once.

7. The itch is not really _____ the bite.

8. All mosquitoes pass _____ their early stages _____ or _____ water.

9. Mosquito eggs will not hatch _____ water.

10. They pollinate flowers as they fly _____ one _____ the other.

E. Determiners: Write any appropriate determiner in the blanks below. If no determiner is necessary, write an "*X*" in the blank.

_____ next time _____ mosquito bites you, just
(1)   (2)
remember that you were chosen. If _____ mosquito likes you, she
(3)
settles onto _____ flesh, and she breaks _____ skin with
(4)   (5)
_____ proboscis tip. It's _____ kind of _____
(6)   (7)   (8)
mouth, and it sticks out just below _____ mosquito's eyes. It
(9)
contains _____ six sharp instruments called _____ stylets.
(10)   (11)
She stabs _____ all six stylets into _____ skin at
(12)   (13)
_____ once. If she hits _____ blood vessel, she'll get
(14)   (15)
_____ full dinner in about _____ minute.
(16)   (17)

F. **Antonyms: Each sentence contains two opposite words. Circle the word that completes the sentence correctly.**

1. Women are (male–female). Men are (male–female).

2. On a humid day, there is a lot of (moisture–dryness) in the air.

3. Please (reject–accept) my apologies for being late.

4. Mosquitoes won't bite just anyone. They look for someone (ordinary–special).

5. If you (separate–mix) all the pencils, you will have one stack of red pencils and one stack of blue ones.

6. When I drink soda, I like to (suck it up–spit it out) through a straw.

7. The fire (produced–destroyed) two houses and caused lots of damage.

8. Alfonso (no longer–still) lives on First Avenue. He moved to Fourth Avenue two months ago.

9. Many people like to (use up–store) some food in case of an emergency.

10. (Ouch!–Aah!). That feels good!

G. **Word Forms: Choose the correct word form to fit into each sentence. Use appropriate verb tenses, singular or plural forms for nouns, and passive voice where necessary.**

1. **to ensure, sure, surely**
   a. _____ you don't believe that story!
   b. Emilio is _____ to succeed at whatever he tries.
   c. What can you do to _____ that you will stay healthy?

2. **fortune, misfortune, fortunate, fortunately, unfortunate, unfortunately**
   a. It has been my good _____ to know the De Palma family.
   b. Mr. and Mrs. De Palma are _____ to have three wonderful children.
   c. _____ , all of the children are very smart.
   d. _____ , one of them just broke her arm in an accident.
   e. It was her _____ to fall down a flight of stairs.
   f. What an _____ experience!

3. **sense, sensor, sensation, sensitivity, to sense, sensitive, sensitively**
   a. Many animals have whiskers or antennae that act as _____ .
   b, I feel a strange _____ in my right leg.
   c. Mr. Kolpacoff has an excellent _____ of humor.
   d. My friend listened very _____ to my problems.
   e. She showed great _____ in her suggestions for what I could do.
   f. Some people are extremely _____ to wool, and can't wear wool clothing.
   g. As soon as he walked into the room, the detective _____ that something was wrong.

4. **moisture, to moisten, moist**
   a. _____ the sponge before you wash the dishes.
   b. Certain plants need lots of _____ to grow well.
   c. The doctor said that my sore throat would get better if I keep the air _____ .

5. **warmth, to warm, warm, warmly**
   a. It's too _____ in here; please turn down the heat.
   b. The waitress greeted us _____ when we entered the restaurant.
   c. For dinner tonight, I'm just going to _____ up some leftovers.
   d. Nothing feels as good as the _____ of a fire on a cold night.

6. **appetite, appetizer, appetizing**
   a. Whenever I get sick, I lose my _____ .
   b. What kind of _____ did they serve before dinner at the party?
   c. That food doesn't look very _____ . I don't think I want any.

7. **specialist, specialty/specialization, to specialize, special, especially**
   a. I made this cake _____ for you.
   b. I made it from a _____ recipe that my grandmother gave me.
   c. Dr. Wilson's _____ is brain surgery.
   d. He is a brain _____ .
   e. He _____ in surgery when he went to medical school.

8. **sharpness, sharpener, to sharpen, sharp, sharply**
   a. Mr. Chen took an evening course to _____ his accounting skills.
   b. The mother spoke _____ to the naughty child.
   c. A knife with a _____ edge cuts very easily.
   d. That pencil _____ will really put a good point on your pencil.
   e. Test the _____ of the needle before you use it.

9. **mixture, mix, mix-up, to mix, mixed**
   a. Do you like to eat _____ vegetables?
   b. What color do you get if you _____ red and yellow?
   c. I'm afraid there's been a _____ . My appointment is at 9 a.m.
   d. It's easy to bake a cake using a cake _____ .
   e. A _____ of tea and honey is good for a sore throat.

10. **store, storage, to store, stored**
    a. When I moved from a large house to a small apartment, I had to put many things in _____ .
    b. Where is the nearest shoe _____ ?
    c. Squirrels _____ nuts during the summer to eat in the winter.
    d. They live through the winter on this _____ food.

H. Sentence Scramble: Make a sentence out of each group of words.

1. mosquito – are – with – acquainted – the – you

2. chooses – carefully – her – she – victims

3. it – mosquito's – out – just – below – eyes – sticks – the

4. lay – will – during – time – she – this – eggs – four or five times

5. mosquitoes – on – flowers – male – of – nectar – live – the

I. Topics for Discussion and Composition:

1. If you could live in an environment with no insects, would you choose to do so? Why? Why not? Please give several reasons for your position and illustrate your reasons with specific examples.

2. Pretend that you are a mosquito and write about a typical day in your life.

3. Write about human beings from a mosquito's point of view. Describe the good points and the bad points of human beings. Explain why nature made human beings.

4. Chemicals that destroy insects injure all living things. Are you in favor of prohibiting insect-killing chemicals such as DDT? Why? Or why not? Please give several reasons for your position and illustrate your reasons with specific examples.

5. Insects are often annoying, but they are necessary. Go to a library and look up information about insects in an encyclopedia. Then, write a composition about the positive role insects play in nature.

J. **Reading Reconstruction: Read this paragraph as many times as you can in three minutes. Then, with your book closed, try to restate the ideas as clearly and completely as you can. (See Chapter 1 for complete instructions.)**

Mosquitoes

Mosquitoes are all over the world. Fortunately, most mosquitoes have an appetite for animals, birds, and even other insects. Only certain species bite people. However, if a mosquito finds you appetizing, she may bite you several times, or she may pick several people to bite. She can store 15 to 20 bites, which all together equal one drop of water. Although mosquitoes are no longer a serious health problems in most countries, they can be annoying. If you have a mosquito problem, remember that they reproduce in water. Be sure to eliminate these spots in and around your home. The smallest amount of water—in an empty can, a flower vase, or an old tire—can produce hundreds of mosquitoes.

Key words (to be written on the chalkboard):

fortunately	appetizing	annoying
appetite	pick	reproduce
insects	store	eliminate
certain	drop	flower vase
species	no longer	old tire

K. Comprehension Check: On a separate piece of paper, write the numbers 1 through 10 on both sides. Mark one side "Test 1" and the other side "Test 2." Read each statement and decide whether it is true or false. Write "T" after true statements and "F" after false statements under Test 1. After you have finished the comprehension check, turn Test 1 face down. Then read the article again and do the comprehension check again under Test 2. Base your answers on the information in this article *only*, even if you disagree with what the author said.

1. Mosquitoes live all over the world.

2. Both male and female mosquitoes bite.

3. Mosquitoes need blood to reproduce.

4. Mosquitoes bite the first person they find.

5. Before they bite, mosquitoes test your body warmth, moisture, and chemical substances.

6. Mosquito bites itch from the saliva that the mosquito mixes with your blood.

7. Mosquitoes need many drops of blood to produce hundreds of eggs.

8. Mosquito eggs need water in order to hatch.

9. Mosquito eggs will die if they don't get water right away.

10. Nature created mosquitoes just to annoy people.

Review Examination I (Chapters 1, 2, 3, 4)

A. **Prepositions and Verb-Completers: Write any appropriate preposition or verb-completer in the blank spaces. (20 points: 1 point each.)**

1. Tribalism is one _____ the most difficult customs _____ understand.

2. Eight _____ the posts were filled _____ Kikuyus.

3. What accounts _____ this ability _____ survive _____ such old age?

4. _____ a great extent, they are separated _____ the pressures _____ industrial society.

5. You are acquainted _____ the mosquito.

6. If you don't appeal _____ her, she'll reject you _____ someone else.

7. She stabs all six stylets _____ you _____ once.

8. One _____ _____ seven people lives _____ a desert area.

9. Their existence is threatened _____ the slow spread _____ the deserts.

B. Word Forms: Look at the first word in each line. Write the appropriate form of this word in the sentence that follows it. Be careful to use appropriate verb tenses, singular and plural forms for nouns, and passive voice where necessary. (50 points: 2 points each.)

(Example)

evidence: It is ___*evident*___ that you studied.

1. **manage:** May I please speak to the _____ ?

2. **force:** The president spoke very _____ .

3. **sense:** That was a very _____ thing to do.

4. **thoughtful:** Do you ever _____ about your country?

5. **evidence:** _____ , Mrs. Vila arrived early.

6. **divisive:** There was a serious _____ between the two groups.

7. **celebrate:** We _____ his birthday last Saturday.

8. **pass:** How many _____ were on the bus?

9. **industry:** Germany is a major _____ nation.

10. **intention:** I called you so early _____ .

11. **worry:** You look very _____ .

12. **similarly:** There are many _____ between us.

13. **sure:** Miss Schwartz will _____ succeed.

14. **fortunate:** He made a _____ when he was young.

15. **warmth:** It's terribly _____ in here.

16. **specialize:** My son wants _____ in mathematics.

17. **sharpener:** That knife has a _____ edge.

18. **mixture:** Can you _____ oil and water?

19. **dried:** The earth became so _____ that nothing grew.

20. **fail:** He thought he was a _____ because he never got rich.

21. **populated:** What is the _____ of London?

22. **dependent:**   I usually _____ on my dictionary when I don't know a word.

23. **protective:**   What is the best _____ against a cold?

24. **add:**   I don't like coffee. _____ I don't like tea.

25. **planner:**   Mr. Lee _____ to get a new job.

C. Synonyms: From this list, choose a synonym for the word in bold type in the sentences below. (20 points: 2 points each.)

add to	clearly	power
answer	delicate	surprising
area	point	very large
chose		

1. A policeman has the **authority** to give you a traffic ticket.

2. Please **reply** by next Wednesday.

3. The Tokyo **region** is very crowded.

4. Fruits and vegetables **contribute to** a good diet.

5. I heard a **remarkable** story yesterday.

6. I **picked** the nicest suit to wear to the party.

7. Mosquitoes bite with the **tip** of their proboscis.

8. Deserts cover a **vast** region.

9. I can see the mountains **distinctly** in the distance.

10. The desert soil is **fragile.**

D. Punctuation: Write in capital letters, periods, and commas where needed. (10 points: 1 point each.)

in some regions of the soviet union nearly 50 out of every 100,000 people live to celebrate their 100th birthday by comparison in america only 3 people in 100,000 reach 100 what accounts for their ability to survive to such old age?

It's delicious—but is it nutritious?

5

TEST YOUR NUTRITION IQ

[All of us eat every day, but most of us don't understand nutrition. How much do you know about good nutrition? Please answer these twelve questions based on current ideas about food and health. The answers may surprise you.]

A.   How much do you know about **nutrition**? If your knowledge is similar to that of food shoppers who answered three **surveys** for the U.S. Food and Drug Administration, then you probably share some widespread misinformation about nutrition. Are the following statements true or false?

 good diet

 questionnaires

 1. *You'll get proper nourishment if you just eat a variety of foods.*
False. Variety is not a guarantee of good nutrition. But adults can generally get a balanced diet by including several servings daily from the four main food groups: two or more from the *milk* group (milk, cheese, yogurt, and other dairy foods); two or more from the *meat* group (meat, poultry, fish, eggs, and meat alternates such as dried beans, lentils, and nuts); four or more from the *bread* group (bread, cereal, noodles, rice, and other grain products); four or more from the *vegetables and fruit* group.

 2. *People who don't eat meat or fish can still stay healthy.*
True. As long as people eat enough dairy foods, eggs, and meat alternates, they can get **essential** protein.

 necessary

 3. *Food eaten between meals can be just as good for health as food eaten at regular meals.*
True. Nutritional value depends on what types of food you eat, not when you eat them. Eating a hard-boiled egg or an orange as a snack can contribute to a well-balanced diet.

4. *Fresh vegetables cooked at home are always more nutritious than canned or frozen vegetables.*
False. The nutritional difference depends more on how vegetables are handled or prepared than in whether they are bought fresh or packaged. Overcooking, for example, destroys many nutrients. Vegetables cooked in too much water can lose a significant amount of vitamins.

5. *A high-protein, low-carbohydrate diet is ideal for losing weight.*
False. There's nothing magical about protein. The simple truth is that you have to either eat fewer calories or use up more in order to lose weight. Yet one of the most common myths about weight control is that carbohydrates, not too many calories, make fat.

6. *When dieting, avoid starchy foods, such as bread or potatoes.*
False. If you cut out starchy foods, such as peas, potatoes, bread, and rice, you cut out very good sources of several B vitamins, Vitamin C, and other nutrients. Moreover, ounce for ounce, bread and potatoes have fewer calories than sirloin steak and roast beef.

7. *If you weigh what you should, you're getting proper nourishment.*
False. Proper weight alone doesn't show whether a diet is lacking in vitamins and minerals. The scales make no distinction between the similar number of calories of a can of low-nutrition soda and two eggs, but body chemistry does.

8. *Taking extra vitamins beyond the recommended daily allowances won't give you more energy.*
True. It's widely believed that extra vitamins provide more energy. But taking more than the body needs doesn't make it function better, any more than overfilling your gas tank makes your car run better.

9. *Natural vitamins are better supplements for the diet than synthetic vitamins.*

man-made

False. There is no difference. A vitamin has the same properties and specific chemical structure whether made in a laboratory or taken from plant or animal parts.

10. *Older people need the same amount of vitamins as younger people.*
True. Older people need the same amount of vitamins as younger people although they need fewer calories. Certain illnesses raise the requirements for some vitamins, but that is true for the young as well as the old.

11. *Food grown in poor, worn-out soil is lower in vitamins than food grown in rich soil.*
False. The vitamins in our foods are made by the plants themselves. They don't come from the soil. However, the *minerals* in a plant depend on the minerals in the soil.

12. *Food produced with chemical fertilizers is just as nutritious as food grown with natural fertilizers.*
True. So-called "natural" fertilizers such as manure must first be broken down by soil bacteria into basic compounds. These compounds, taken up by the plant, are identical whether they come from natural or from chemical fertilizers.

B.   If you answered at least eight of the questions correctly, you can consider yourself well informed about food and nutrition by today's standards. But remember that nutrition is a complex and growing science, and that today's beliefs may be changed as new information becomes available.

TURN TO COMPREHENSION CHECK AT END OF CHAPTER

READING TIMES:
1st reading _____ minutes
2nd reading_____ minutes

READING SPEED:
7 minutes = 101 wpm
6 minutes = 118 wpm
5 minutes = 141 wpm
4 minutes = 176 wpm
3 minutes = 235 wpm

A. **Analysis of Ideas and Relationships: Circle the letter next to the best answer.**

1. According to paragraph A,
   a. many people have incorrect ideas about nutrition.
   b. most people are well informed about nutrition.
   c. many people don't care about nutrition.

2. According to paragraph 1, what is a "meat alternate"? How do you know?
   a. Dried beans.
   b. Fish.
   c. Milk.

3. According to paragraph 4, which statement is **not** true in regard to nutrition?
   a. Overcooking destroys many nutrients.
   b. Both fresh and frozen vegetables are nutritious.
   c. It makes no difference how you prepare vegetables.

4. According to paragraph 6,
   a. bread and steak have the same number of calories per ounce.
   b. starchy foods are unnecessary in a balanced diet.
   c. you should include starchy foods in your diet.

5. According to paragraph 7,
   a. a can of soda and two eggs have a similar number of calories.
   b. a can of soda and two eggs are nutritionally similar.
   c. a can of soda and two eggs make a good snack.

6. In paragraph 8, the description of "overfilling your gas tank" shows:
   a. why you should take extra vitamins.
   b. why you don't need extra vitamins.
   c. why extra vitamins cost more.

7. In paragraph 10, the word "raise" means:
   a. take care of.
   b. increase.
   c. get more money.

8. In paragraph 10, "but that is true for the young as well as the old," **young** refers to:
   a. illnesses.
   b. people.
   c. vitamins.

9. In paragraph 11, the word "rich" means:
   a. fertile.
   b. wealthy.
   c. heavy.

10. A good title for this article would be:
    a. Nutrition: A Complex, Growing Science
    b. How to Lose Weight
    c. What You Should Know about Nutrition

B. Interpretation of Words and Phrases: Circle the letter next to the best answer.

1. Eating a hard-boiled egg as a **snack** can contribute to a well-balanced diet.
   a. diet food
   b. small meal between regular meals
   c. large meal at lunchtime

2. Nutritional value **depends on** how the vegetables are cooked.
   a. is based on
   b. has nothing to do with
   c. looks into

3. You must **use up** more calories in order to lose weight.
   a. throw away
   b. consume
   c. collect

4. **Yet**, many people think carbohydrates make fat.
   a. later
   b. I agree
   c. however

5. If you **cut out** starchy foods, you cut out good sources of nutrients.
   a. eliminate
   b. use a knife on
   c. eat

6. **Moreover**, bread and potatoes have fewer calories per ounce than steak.
   a. heavier
   b. away
   c. also

7. Food grown in **worn-out** soil is not lower in vitamins.
   a. well cared for
   b. deteriorated
   c. outdoors

8. Fertilizers must first be **broken down** by bacteria.
   a. separated into smaller pieces
   b. grown to larger size
   c. discovered

9. These compounds are **taken up** by the plant.
   a. collected
   b. studied
   c. destroyed

10. Consider yourself **well informed** about food.
    a. uninformed
    b. healthy
    c. knowledgeable

C. **Synonyms: From this list, choose a synonym for the word in bold type in each sentence.**

artificial	limit	supplier
characteristics	principal	treat
exactly the same	see no difference	well-distributed
extensive		

1. You probably share some **widespread** misinformation about nutrition.

2. Everyone should eat a **balanced** diet.

3. Include several servings from the four **main** food groups.

4. **Handle** vegetables carefully.

5. It isn't easy to **control** your weight.

6. Potatoes are a good **source** of vitamin C.

7. The scales **make no distinction** between the calories in a can of soda and in two eggs.

8. There is no difference between natural vitamins and **synthetic** vitamins.

9. Natural and synthetic vitamins have the same **properties**.

10. These compounds are **identical** whether they come from natural or chemical fertilizers.

D. Prepositions and Verb-Completers: Write any appropriate preposition or verb-completer in the blank spaces.

1. How much do you know _____ nutrition?

2. You can get a balanced diet _____ including foods _____ the four main food groups.

3. Nutritional value depends _____ what types _____ food you eat.

4. Overcooking, _____ example, destroys many nutrients.

5. Vegetables cooked _____ too much water can lose a significant amount _____ vitamins.

6. You have _____ eat fewer calories or use _____ more _____ order _____ lose weight.

7. Is your diet lacking _____ vitamins?

8. Are natural vitamins better _____ the diet than synthetic vitamins?

9. Vitamins don't come _____ the soil. They are made _____ the plants themselves.

10. Consider yourself well informed _____ food if you answered _____ least eight _____ the questions correctly.

E. **Determiners: Write any appropriate determiner in the blanks below. If no determiner is necessary, write an "X" in the blank.**

Variety is not _____ guarantee of _____ good
                 (1)   (2)

nutrition. But _____ adults can generally get _____
              (3)   (4)

balanced diet by including several _____ servings daily from
                        (5)

_____ four main food groups. There's nothing magical about
   (6)

_____ protein. _____ simple truth is that you either have
   (7)   (8)

to eat _____ fewer _____ calories or use up _____
       (9)   (10)   (11)

more in order to lose _____ weight. One of _____ most
              (12)   (13)

common _____ myths about _____ weight control is that
        (14)   (15)

_____ carbohydrates, not too many _____ calories, make
   (16)   (17)

_____ fat.
   (18)

F. **Antonyms: Each sentence contains two opposite words. Circle the word that completes the sentence correctly.**

1. Cotton is a (natural–synthetic) material.

2. That (fresh–old) fish smells terrible!

3. If you want to drive, it is (unnecessary–essential) to have a driver's license.

4. The wooden building was completely (destroyed–constructed) by the fire.

5. If you use (complex–simple) words, I can understand you.

6. If you (keep–use up) all your money now, you won't have any for emergencies.

7. I already have a (general–specific) idea about the problem, but I don't know all the details.

8. This coat is (worn out–in good condition). I can wear it for a few more years.

9. There is a great (similarity–difference) in our political beliefs. We agree on most things.

10. It is a (myth–fact) that you can stay healthy even if you don't eat meat.

G. **Word Forms: Choose the correct word form to fit into each sentence. Use appropriate verb tenses, singular or plural forms for nouns, and passive voice where necessary.**

1. **nutrition, nutrient, nutritionist, nutritious, nutritiously**
   a. The _____ told me how to get a balanced diet.
   b. The _____ in potatoes are good for you.
   c. Good _____ depends on eating a balanced diet.
   d. What is the most _____ food?
   e. If you plan meals _____ , you will stay healthy.

2. **knowledge, to know, knowledgeable, knowledgeably**
   a. To my _____ , such a thing has never happened.
   b. Paul is very _____ about automobiles.
   c. He _____ how to fix any kind of car.
   d. He speaks _____ about all kinds of cars.

3. **information, to inform, informative, informatively**
   a. I read a very _____ article about Egypt.
   b. The article had lots of interesting _____ .
   c. The newspaper always _____ me about world events.
   d. The author wrote _____ about conditions in Egypt.

4. **regularity, regular, regularly**
   a. Mr. Keller _____ takes the 8 a.m. train to work.
   b. Going to work is part of his _____ schedule.
   c. He also likes to exercise with _____ .

5. **value, to value, valuable**
   a. Is there anything more _____ than gold?
   b. If you _____ your health, you will take care of yourself.
   c. What is the _____ of that diamond ring?

6. **freshness, to freshen, fresh, freshly**
   a. Always check for _____ before you buy fish.
   b. After I get home from school, I like to _____ up with a shower before cooking dinner.
   c. I love to eat _____ picked tomatoes.
   d. The smell of _____ coffee is delicious.

7. **avoidance, to avoid, avoidable, unavoidable**
   a. The accident was _____ because the child ran into the street so suddenly.
   b. If you have high blood pressure, you should _____ eating salt.
   c. The _____ of salt is important if your blood pressure is high.
   d. Salty foods are _____ if you shop carefully.

8. **recommendation, to recommend**
   a. My teacher gave me a letter of _____ when I graduated.
   b. This book on nutrition _____ that you eat some vegetables every day.

9. **nature, natural, naturally**
   a. Can you get a good diet _____ if you eat a variety of foods?
   b. Miss Yee has never taken any painting lessons but she has a _____ ability to paint.
   c. I learned a lot about _____ because I grew up on a farm.

10. **break, to break, broken, breakable**
    a. There was a _____ in the clouds and the sun came out.
    b. Don't _____ any of the dishes.
    c. Since glass dishes are _____ , handle them carefully.
    d. John suffered four _____ bones in the accident.

H. Sentence Scramble: Make a sentence out of each group of words.

1. you – nutrition – much – know – do – how – about – ?

2. is – of – good – not – a – guarantee – nutrition – variety

3. nutritional – value – of – eat – on – depends – what – food – types – you

4. nothing – protein – there's – about – magical

5. science – nutrition – complex – is – and – a – growing

I. Topics for Discussion and Composition

1. Paragraph 1 of this article says that people should eat a variety of foods from the four main food groups. In different countries, people typically eat different foods from these groups. For example, people in Asia generally eat rice, while Europeans generally eat bread and potatoes. Describe the foods that make up the typical diet in your native country from the four groups: milk, meat, bread, and vegetables and fruit. Then describe some typical meals using these foods.

2. In every country, people think that certain foods are especially good or bad for their health. There are also some foods that are eaten for special reasons or by certain people (for example: by sick people, children, old people; to become strong, to stay youthful, etc.). Describe some of the foods that people eat for special reasons in your native country. Are there any reasons why they feel this way about these foods? (For example: the food contains large amounts of certain vitamins or minerals, it grows in very rich soil, etc.).

3. If you could meet all your nutritional needs by simply taking a pill every day (and not eating), would you do this? Why? Or why not? Please give reasons for your position and illustrate your reasons with examples.

4. Material needs (food, shelter, clothing) are more important than mental and spiritual needs. Do you agree or disagree? Why? Please give reasons for your position and illustrate your reasons with examples.

5. If you had to choose only three food items (for example, bread, apples, milk) to live on for the rest of your life, what would you choose? Why?

6. People disagree about which is more important for health: nutrition or exercise. Which do you believe is more important? Why? Please give reasons to support your position and illustrate your reasons with examples.

7. Write a story and include this sentence someplace in your story: "Oh, one more little piece of cake won't matter," she said.

J. Reading Reconstruction: Read this paragraph as many times as you can in three minutes. Then, with your book closed, try to restate the ideas as clearly and completely as you can. (See Chapter 1 for complete instructions.)

How to Lose Weight

A humorist once wrote that the word "diet" (to lose weight) comes from the verb "to die." Most people who try to lose weight would probably agree. In the United States, being overweight is a widespread problem. Nutritionists have many recommendations to help people control their weight. One current method is to have people make a distinction between real hunger and other factors that make them eat. For example, a traveling salesman realized that he ate lots of snacks only while driving his car. Now he avoids keeping any food in his car. Since he found the source of his overeating, he can handle the problem.

Key words (to be written on the chalkboard):

humorist	control	snacks
lose weight	current	avoids
widespread	make a distinction	source
nutritionists	factors	handle
recommendation	salesman	

K. Comprehension Check: On a separate piece of paper, write the numbers
    1 through 10 on both sides. Mark one side "Test 1" and the other side
    "Test 2." Read each statement and decide whether it is true or false.
    Write "T" after true statements and "F" after false statements under
    Test 1. After you have finished the comprehension check, turn Test 1
    face down. Then read the article again and do the comprehension check
    again under Test 2. Base your answers on the information in this article
    only, even if you disagree with what the author said.

1. Most people have a lot of misinformation about nutrition.

2. There are four main food groups.

3. Eating a variety of foods is a guarantee of good nutrition.

4. You can eat meat alternates instead of meat.

5. You should not eat snacks between meals.

6. Carbohydrates make fat.

7. Starchy foods are good sources of several B vitamins.

8. Ounce for ounce, bread is more fattening than steak.

9. Older people need fewer calories than younger people.

10. Scientists today still do not know everything about nutrition.

6

MEXICO'S PASSIONATE AFFAIR WITH THE COMICS

[Comic books are popular around the world, but they are unusually popular in Mexico. This article discusses the role of comic books in Mexico and some of the different points of view about comics in this country.]

1   **Slumped** in parked police cars, riding crowded buses, having their shoes cleaned, hidden behind fruit stalls in a market, or just standing expressionless on the street, millions of Mexicans live double lives. Their hidden passion may be Kaliman, the "incredible man" who uses his great physical and mental powers to defend the weak. It may be Anahi, the **natural** daughter of a French aristocrat and a Latin bandido who uses her beauty and courage to fight the local dictatorship. It may be one of dozens of other heroes and heroines who appear in comic books every week.

bent over

illegitimate

2   Statistics are difficult to find, but industry sources believe that more comic books are consumed per capita in Mexico than in any other Latin American country. However, *El Heraldo de México*, the daily newspaper with the largest circulation, says it prints 200,000 copies of its paper each day; yet, "Kaliman" and "Tears, Laughter and Love" (two of the most popular comic books) sell 1.3 million copies a week—each—for about 10 cents a copy.

3   The publishers of "Tears, Laughter and Love" produce 16 other comic books with total sales of more than four million. In addition, about five million other comic books are sold here every week—with each copy passed around to many readers.

favorite

4   The stories are carefully written for a mass audience that is openly sentimental. A few years ago, "Doctor Heart" was a great **hit** with such problems as "I was married to an invalid but loved another," "My sister stole my husband," and "Should I tell my son who his true father is?" Now, many comic books are set in different countries or periods. The best seller "Fire"

tells

recounts the adventures of the 19th century black ruler of Haiti, Henri Christophe, for example. But these comics still involve the melodramatic conflicts of family and love no matter where or when they take place.

5   Significantly, such translated imports from the United States as "Donald Duck," "Superman," and "Batman" have never been as popular as their locally written competitors—perhaps because North American passion seems too mild to Latins.

6   Many leftists believe that most comic books are harmful to society. "They try to entertain with idiotic stories and with the lowest forms of sex and violence and cheap melodrama," said Eduardo del Río, who, under the name "Ruis," is Mexico's best-known political cartoonist. "The comic books are of a very poor cultural level and rarely try to encourage the reader to use his imagination."

insisted
invented

7   He **maintained** that the prosperous publishers had **made up** the rationalization that they were helping readers toward literacy. "This is entirely false," he said. "The comic books are totally alienating. They give people something to do without thinking—a sort of consolation for their poverty."

8   Mr. del Río believes, however, that comic books remain a valuable form of communication, and for more than a decade, he has been publishing a series

bent over

called "Los Agachados" ("The **Stooped** Ones"), which deals with serious social and political issues. With a

dealt with

circulation of 120,000, "Los Agachados" has **tackled** such themes as government repression, guerrilla movements, inflation, and corruption.

9   Increasingly, the political **potential** of comic   possibilities
books is being recognized. Leftist parties have adopted
them to carry their message to poor peasants and
workers, often using simple stories and drawings to
explain the meaning of such terms as "Marxism" and
"imperialism." The government has also turned to
comic books to promote its programs, particularly its
nationwide campaign for family planning.

10   "There's nothing wrong with the medium," Mr.
del Río noted. "Comic books can be good or bad. It's
just a question of how they're used."

TURN TO COMPREHENSION CHECK AT END OF CHAPTER

READING TIMES: READING SPEED:
1st reading _____ minutes   6 minutes = 100 wpm
2nd reading _____ minutes   5 minutes = 120 wpm
                              4 minutes = 150 wpm
                              3 minutes = 201 wpm

A. Analysis of Ideas and Relationships: Circle the letter next to the best answer.

1. The subject of this article is:
   a. Mexico.
   b. comic books.
   c. the popularity of comic books in Mexico.

2. "Kaliman" and "Tears, Laughter and Love" together sell:
   a. almost twice as many copies as *El Heraldo de México* does each week.
   b. almost as many copies as *El Heraldo de México* does each week.
   c. half as many copies as *El Heraldo de México* does each week.

3. How many comic books are sold in Mexico each week according to this article?
   a. About nine million.
   b. About 11.6 million.
   c. About five million.

4. Compared with North American comics, Mexican comics are:
   a. much more passionate.
   b. more intellectual.
   c. cold and reserved.

   Please explain your answer.

5. Leftists such as Eduardo del Río:
   a. do not approve of the popular mass-audience comics.
   b. do not approve of any comics.
   c. approve of comic books because they help people learn to read better.

   Please explain your answer.

6. "Los Agachados" is an example of a:
   a. silly, sentimental comic book.
   b. social-political comic book.
   c. melodramatic 19th century adventure comic book.

7. Leftist parties like comic books because they believe that:
   a. comics can be a useful way of carrying political messages to poor peasants and workers.
   b. comics give people something to do without thinking, and they offer poor people a sort of consolation for their poverty.
   c. comic books are very engaging and entertaining, and they offer people welcome diversion from everyday concerns.

8. The Mexican government:
   a. has used comic books to promote some of its social programs.
   b. strongly disapproves of comic books and is thinking of outlawing them.
   c. is the chief publisher of comic books in Mexico.

9. Which statement best represents the tone of this article?
   a. Comic books are good.
   b. Comic books are bad.
   c. Comic books can be good or bad. It's just a question of how they're used.

10. This article is:
    a. an objective picture of comic books in Mexico.
    b. a negative picture of comic books in Mexico.
    c. an enthusiastic picture of comic books in Mexico.

    Please explain your answer.

B. Interpretation of Words and Phrases: Circle the letter next to the best answer.

1. "Millions of Mexicans **live double lives.**"
   a. They work as spies.
   b. They have split personalities.
   c. They have a strong fantasy life in addition to their regular, everyday life.

2. "Industry sources believe that more comic books **are consumed per capita** in Mexico than in any other Latin American country."
   a. are eaten per person
   b. are read per person
   c. are digested per person

3. "Each copy is passed around to many readers."
   a. Many people read each copy.
   b. Each person has his own copy.
   c. People pass around copies to each other, but they don't read them.

4. "I was married to an invalid but loved another." This means that "I" loved:
   a. another invalid.
   b. another person, presumably not an invalid.
   c. no one.

5. "My sister stole my husband." This means that:
   a. my sister kidnapped my husband.
   b. my sister stole things from my husband.
   c. my sister got my husband to fall in love with her instead of me.

6. "The comic books are of a very poor cultural level and **rarely** try to encourage the reader to use his imagination."
   a. hardly ever
   b. really
   c. often

7. "The prosperous publishers had made up the rationalization that they were helping readers toward literacy."
   a. The successful, well-to-do publishers invented the excuse that their comic books were helping people learn how to read better.
   b. The successful, well-to-do publishers invented the excuse that they were helping their readers understand the meaning of literacy.
   c. The successful, well-to-do publishers invented the excuse that they were helping good readers to become literate.

8. "**Increasingly**, the political potential of comic books is being recognized."
   a. little by little
   b. more and more
   c. slowly

9. "There's nothing wrong with the **medium**."
   a. middle position
   b. communication form
   c. average

10. "The government has also **turned to** comic books to promote its programs."
   a. used
   b. looked at
   c. moved toward

11. "Comic books can be good or bad. **It's just a question of how they're used**."
   a. Do you have a question about how they are used?
   b. It depends on how they are used.
   c. I question how they are used.

C. Synonyms: From this list, choose a synonym for the word in bold type in each sentence.

full of false emotion	very popular
tell stories about	large and unspecialized
bend over	stupid
share them	try to do
for each person	to get along with

1. Please sit up straight; don't **slump over** like that, or you will have bad posture.

2. What is the annual income in Mexico **per capita**?

3. I only have a few copies of these magazines so please **pass them around** so that everyone can see them.

4. That story was too **sentimental** for my taste.

5. "Gone with the Wind" has been **a great hit** since it was first released in 1939.

6. If you think that problem is too easy, why don't you **tackle** this one?

7. It is difficult to know how **to deal with** him when he's in a bad mood.

8. Most comic books are written for a **mass** audience.

9. Some of the comic book stories are **idiotic**.

10. He loved to **recount** his war experiences to anyone who would listen.

D. Prepositions and Verb-Completers: Write any appropriate preposition or verb-completer in the blank spaces.

1. Millions _____ Mexicans read comic books.

2. More comic books are read _____ Mexico than _____ any other Latin American country.

3. Two _____ the most popular comic books are "Kaliman" and "Tears, Laughter and Love."

4. The stories are written _____ a mass audience that is openly sentimental.

5. Now, many comic books are set _____ different countries or periods.

6. "Fire" recounts the adventures _____ the 19th century black ruler _____ Haiti, Henri Christophe, _____ example.

7. These comics still involve the melodramatic conflicts _____ family and love.

8. Comic books _____ the United States have never been popular _____ Mexico.

9. Many leftists believe that most comic books are harmful _____ society.

10. There is nothing wrong _____ comic books; it's just a question _____ how they are used.

E. Cloze Exercise: Fill in the blanks with any appropriate word.

Statistics are difficult to _____ , but industry sources believe
(1)
_____ more comic books are _____ per capita in Mexico
(2)   (3)
_____ in any other Latin _____ country. However, *El*
(4)   (5)
Heraldo de México, _____ daily newspaper with the _____
(6)   (7)
circulation, says it prints 200,000 _____ of its paper each
(8)
_____ ; yet, "Kaliman" and "Tears, Laughter and Love"
(9)
(_____ of the most popular _____ books) sell 1.3 million
(10)   (11)
copies _____ week—each—for about 10 _____ a copy.
(12)   (13)

F. Punctuation Exercise: Write in capital letters, periods, and commas where needed.

the publishers of "tears laughter and love" produce 16 other comic books with total sales of more than four million in addition about five million other comic books are sold here every week—with each copy passed around to many readers

the stories are carefully written for a mass audience that is openly sentimental a few years ago "doctor heart" was a great hit with such problems as "i was married to an invalid but loved another" "my sister stole my husband" and "should i tell my son who his true father is"

G. **Word Forms: Choose the correct word form to fit into each sentence. Use appropriate verb tenses, singular or plural forms for nouns, and passive voice where necessary.**

1. **to hide, hiding, hidden**
   a. Here is a good _____ place. No one will find it here.
   b. He could not _____ the fact that he was disappointed.
   c. The _____ treasure was recently discovered.

2. **passion, passionate, passionately**
   a. Anyone could see that they were _____ in love with each other.
   b. It was a _____ love affair.
   c. Most crimes are crimes of _____ .

3. **physical, physically**
   a. You should have a _____ examination to make sure that you are all right.
   b. He was better developed _____ than mentally.

4. **dictator, dictatorship, to dictate, dictatorial**
   a. Napoleon was a famous _____ .
   b. He _____ his orders to his staff every morning, and then he rode out and looked over the army.
   c. He fought against the _____ .
   d. His enemies claimed that he was too _____ .

5. **competitor, competition, to compete, competitive**
   a. She was a very _____ person.
   b. Who won the _____ ?
   c. How many _____ were there in the games?
   d. I don't think I can _____ against her because she has had much more experience.

6. **entertainer, entertainment, to entertain, entertaining**
   a. The book is not very good, but it is _____ .
   b. He was a great _____ .
   c. The _____ at that nightclub is wonderful.
   d. How did you _____ your guests?

7. **adoption, to adopt, adopted**
   a. He's an _____ child, but he acts just like his father.
   b. They _____ him when he was a baby.
   c. _____ laws are usually quite strict.

8. **mentality, mental, mentally**
   a. I was not _____ prepared for that experience.
   b. Those people have an odd _____ .
   c. I believe that she suffers from some kind of _____ illness.

9. **totality, total, to total, total, totally**
   a. I admit that I am not right, but I bet that I am not_____ wrong.
   b. Would you please _____ that column of numbers?
   c. You must examine the situation in its _____ , not just a part of it.
   d. The _____ impression was not very good.
   e. Please add up the _____ .

10. **defender, defense, to defend, defensive, defensively**
   a. I think you are being too _____ .
   b. You responded too _____ .
   c. I would _____ you if I could.
   d. Maybe you don't need a _____ .
   e. What is your _____ ?

H. Sentence Scramble: Make a sentence out of each group of words.

1. popular – books – in – Mexico – comic – very – are

2. conflicts – love – and – family – most – stories – of – the – involve – of

3. messages – political – some – comics – have

4. necessarily – comics – not – are – bad

5. depends – on – it – used – how – are – they

I. **Topics for Discussion and Composition:**

1. Comic books are similar to soap operas on television in many ways. Most of the stories are melodramatic and sentimental. And yet millions and millions of people read these comics and watch these soap operas. Why? What is the great attraction? What needs do they fulfill?

2. Please describe your favorite soap opera or comic book. Who are the main characters? What kinds of experiences do they have? Why do you like this soap opera or comic book?

3. "Comic books can be good or bad. It's just a question of how they're used." Please discuss this statement, giving specific examples of (1) how comics can be good and (2) how comics can be bad.

4. Some people believe that comic books can be useful in helping people learn how to read better. Other people believe that comic books are destructive because they usually don't require the reader to do any real thinking. Which is your position? Why? Please give several reasons and specific examples to support your position.

5. Do you think comic books should have serious messages in them? For example, do you think that social or political matters should be discussed through comic book stories? Why? Or why not? Please give several reasons to support your position. If possible, give examples from your own experience or the experience of people you know.

6. What, if anything, do children learn from comics? Please give specific examples wherever you can. When you were a child, what did you learn from comics? Was your life affected in any way by what you learned from comics? If so, how? And why?

7. Would you allow your child to read comic books? Why? Or why not? Please give several reasons and specific examples to support your position.

8. Comic books are more educational than television. Do you agree or disagree with this statement? Why? Please give reasons and specific examples to support your position.

J.   **Reading Reconstruction: Read this paragraph as many times as you can in three minutes. Then, with your book closed, try to restate the ideas as clearly and completely as you can. (See Chapter 1 exercise for complete instructions.)**

Invitation to a Wedding

Today is the big day: Carole Davis is marrying Dr. Jeffrey Parker. This wedding is a bit unusual. You see, Carole and Jeffrey used to be married to each other. Then Carole fell in love with Jeffrey's brother Tom, and she divorced Jeffrey. After Carole and Tom had been married a couple of years, they were in a terrible automobile accident. Carole was badly scarred, and Tom was killed. Carole went to a famous surgeon. He slowly rebuilt her beautiful face, and, meanwhile, they fell in love. Who was this wonderful, handsome doctor? Of course, it was none other than Dr. Jeffrey Parker, Carole's first husband!

Today at least half a million people will witness Carole and Jeffrey's second wedding. It will be on television. On television? Yes. This is a typical television soap opera, and millions of people watch these stormy, sentimental stories every day.

By the way, you are invited to the wedding. It will be on channel 4 at 1 p.m. Please don't miss it. Even though Carole and Jeffrey are blissfully happy today, trouble is lurking just around the corner. (Trouble is always lurking just around the corner on the afternoon soap operas.) See you at the wedding!

Key words (to be written on the chalkboard):

marrying	killed	witness
wedding	surgeon	soap opera
unusual	rebuilt	sentimental
fell in love	wonderful	blissfully
divorced	handsome	trouble
accident	husband	lurking
scarred		

K. Comprehension Check: On a separate piece of paper, write the numbers 1 through 10 on both sides. Mark one side "Test 1" and the other side "Test 2." Read each statement and decide whether it is true or false. Write "T" after true statements and "F" after false statements under Test 1. After you have finished the comprehension check, turn Test 1 face down. Then read the article again and do the comprehension check again under Test 2. Base your answers on the information in this article *only*, even if you disagree with what the author said.

1. Comic books are more popular in Mexico than in any other Latin American country.

2. Mexican comic books tend to be serious and intellectual.

3. Comic books set in different countries or periods are popular.

4. Most Mexican comics involve conflicts of family and love.

5. The most popular comic books in Mexico are "Donald Duck," "Superman," and "Batman."

6. Mexican comic books tend to be more passionate than North American comic books.

7. Publishers of comic books claim that their comic books help people learn to read better.

8. Mexican leftists are opposed to most popular comic books.

9. Some comic books have political or social messages.

10. The Mexican government has used comic books to promote its family planning program.

MATRIMONIALS FOR GROOMS

Panikkar|Nair Match Required for fair, domesticated Panikkar girl twentyfive, living in Delhi. Simple immediate marriage. Write Box 37821 Times of India, New Delhi-2.　　　　D22562-G

Wanted Tall, Handsome, MBBS for beautiful, Indian girl, settled USA, age 25, 156 cms., drawing 17,500 dollar p.a. No bar. Contact with photo. Doctor B. K. Ahuja, Rani Jhansi Road, Ludhiana. Phone 23577.　　　D154|3-G

Kerala Iyer Family Decently settled in USA looking for a Kerala Iyer groom around 25 years for their 19 year old daughter, good looking, well educated accomplished & brought up in a conservative religious household. Boy should be well educated, with good health & clean habits with willingness to settle down in USA. Write with full details to Mr. Iyer, No. 10, Whitter Drive, Searington, New York 11507.　　　D15480-G

A Fair, Handsome, Independent Tamil Iyer boy, 30, looks very young invites correspondence from parents of Iyer girls upto 22. Girl must be not less than 162 cms white or very fair complexioned and must be exceptionally beautiful. No dowry but girls merits only requirement. Boy of a known family and owns flat in posh locality. Earning five figures. Advt is for proper selection only. Although preference for Iyers other South Indians, no bars. Correspond confidentially with complete details to Box K-645-S, Times of India, Bombay.　　　AA7767(CS)-B

Suitable Rajput Match Preferably Defence officer, bank employee, engineer for convent educated M.A., 159 cms., fair girl 23, only daughter. Father, brother Defence officers. Write Box 37800 Times of India, New Delhi-2.　　　D71495-G

Suitable Gursikh Match For Punjabi Arora (non-Sikh but follower of Gurugranth Sahibji) homely, beautiful, slim, girl M.A., 24 years, 155 cms. Decent marriage, respectable family of Cambelpur (Pakistan). Brothers motorcycle distributors in western U.P. Write Box 37845 Times of India, New Delhi-2.　　D22587-G

Wanted Suitable Match From respectable Bisa Agarwal family, (engineer, doctor or gazetted officer preferred) for a M.A., beautiful, smart, slim and homely girl of 24 years, 154 cms. Write Box 37850 Times of India, New Delhi-2.　　　D22579-G

MATRIMONIALS FOR GROOMS

Well Groomed Decently Placed Iyer widower (43) having an 8-year old boy invites matrimonial correspondence from good looking educated women hailing from decent families—widows' no bar. Write Box K 047—S, Times of India, Bombay-400 001.　　　　A32322(C)-B

Wanted Keralite Non Garga fair, slim, musically talented, well versed in household affairs, employed Brahmin bride for veterinarian aged 26, Pooram, employed at Bombay. Reply Box K —692—S, Times of India, Bombay-400 001.　　A33091(C)-B

Wanted Preferably Sikh, Tall, fair, beautiful, talented, intelligent girl, below 21 years from highly cultured, educated family for tall, fair, handsome Sikh B.E. MBA 25 years, high financial status. Son of industrialist, settled in Bombay. Box L 411—S Times of India, Bombay-1.　　　　A33753(CS)-G

MATRIMONIALS FOR BRIDES

Wanted Really Beautiful Bride from respectable family for Kayastha Engineer Ph.D. 167 cm. employed Senior Class-I Central Govt. officer, drawing Rs. 2100/- caste no bar local Lecturer|Doctor preferred. Write Box 37856 Times of India, New Delhi-2.　　　D22605-B

Separate Or Mutual Alliance invited for an employed Nair girl of 22 and her employed brother of 26. Please reply Box K 612—K Times of India, Bombay 400 001.　　　　A32932(C)-B&G

Wanted Suitable Match For A girl B.A. B.Ed., 28, teacher, 450/- Singhal Gotra, white spot over palm and feet, wearing glasses, height 152 cms. Write Box 37908 Times of India, New Delhi-2.　　　　D22647-G

Class One Officer Or Equivalent vegetarian, teetotaller, Brahmin match for Delhi University lecturer Mohyal Brahmin girl 32 years, 164 cms., slim, beautiful, fair. Write Box 37314 Times of India, New Delhi-2.　　DE14900-G

Sikh Match Of Status Defence business, top executive for slim, beautiful, smart, sophisticated, educated divorcee girl 28 years. Write Box 37330 Times of India, New Delhi-2.　　DE22235-G

MATRIMONIALS FOR BRIDES

Match For Catholic Maiden, 165/32; looks much younger; lecturer, smart, well-connected, accomplished, twice abroad for post graduation, seminars, touring. Write Box 37306 Times of India, New Delhi-2.　　DE14911-G

Same Caste Match Wanted For a Maharashtrian Brahmin girl (Goud Saraswat Brahmin) of 32 years, B.A., B.Ed., height 160 cms. wheaty complexion, graduate | post graduate, well settled and having good family background may correspond. Teachers | agriculturists and widower need not write. Box K 033—S Times of India, Bombay 400 001.　　　　B14978(BDA)-G

Matrimonial Correspondence invited from parents of beautiful, fair sweetnatured, talented, highly educated, good English command bride of 20 to 25 years from cultured family for smart, brilliant, foreign qualified, outstanding master of Elec. Engineering and M.B.A. Globe travelled, 26 years, 168 cms., handsome Gupta bachelor, reaching India early October, for ten years. Father United Nations adviser abroad, monthly income five figures. Own modern 2-1|2 storey bungalow South Delhi, no bars. Girls merit principal consideration, opportunities living India abroad. Write with girl's details, possibly horoscope to Box 37772 Times of India, New Delhi-2.　　　DE22541-B

Alliance Invited From Iyer boys professionals | engineers | doctors | scientists for Iyer girl post-graduate, 29, 160 cms., fair attractive horoscope optional. Apply Box K—322—K Times of India, Bombay-440 001.　　　　AA7489(C)-G

Wanted Convent Educated bride for top German Executive 34, posted in India. Write Box 37783, Times of India, New Delhi-2.　　D15414(CS)-B

A Young Senior Officer Aged 29, employed with a chemical organisation and hailing from U.P. Kshatriya Swarankar invites alliance from girls of respectable families. The girl should be a Graduate, tall, fair complexioned and well versed in household work. Kindly correspond with full particulars to Box L 277-S, Times of India, Bombay 400 001.　　A33539(CS)-B

7

MARRIAGE ADVERTISING IN INDIA'S SUNDAY NEWSPAPERS

[In India, parents have traditionally found husbands or wives for their sons and daughters. Today, the parents are using a new technique in their search—advertisements in the Sunday newspapers. In addition to helping young people find suitable marriage partners, these advertisements reflect the changes that are occurring in Indian society.]

1   Every Sunday morning millions of Indians **settle down** with a cup of tea and the special weekend issues of their newspapers, just as Americans do. But here, with the marriage season **approaching**, many of them turn quickly to a Sunday **feature** that is particularly Indian—the columns and columns of marriage advertisements in which young people look for husbands and wives.

relax

coming
specialty

2   "Beautiful Brahman girl wanted for bank officer from well-connected family," one says. "Vegetarian man (doctor, engineer preferred) for church-educated girl with light **complexion**, says another. "Solid 25-year-old, salary four figures, wants tall, charming, educated Punjabi," says a third.

skin color

3   This is a relatively modern change in the **age-old** custom of the arranged marriage. The thousands of advertisements published each week increasingly **reflect** social changes that are coming to this traditional society. For example, although women are still usually described in terms of appearance, or skills in "the wifely arts," information about their earning power is entering more and more of the advertisements. This reflects the arrival in India of the working wife.

traditional

show

person

4   Divorce, which used to be almost unheard of in India, is sometimes now mentioned in the advertisements as in the case of a woman whose advertisement in a New Delhi newspaper explained that she had been "the innocent **party**" when her marriage broke up.

5   Because the custom of the dowry (marriage payment) is now illegal, some advertisements say "no dowry," or "simple marriage," which means the same thing. However, the fathers of many bridegrooms still require it.

strict

6   As a sign of the slight loosening of the **rigid** caste (social class) system, a number of advertisements promise "caste not important," or "girl's abilities will be main consideration." The majority of them, however, still require not only caste, such as Brahman or Kshatriya, but also a certain home region or ethnic origin.

7   In a land where light skin is often regarded as socially preferable, many also require that a woman have a "wheat-color" complexion or that a man be "tall, fair and handsome."

8   Advertisements are placed and eagerly read by a wide range of people in the upper classes, mostly in cities. Many of them receive dozens of answers. "There's nothing embarrassing about it," explained a Calcutta businessman advertising for a son-in-law. "It's just another way of broadening the contacts and increasing the possibility of doing the best one can for one's daughter."

level

9   Because of high unemployment and a generally poor **standard** of living here, one of the best attractions a marriage advertisement can offer is a permit to live abroad, especially in Canada or the United States. A person who has one can get what he wants.

10   One recent Sunday in Madras, for example, a Punjabi engineer living in San Francisco advertised for a "beautiful slim bride with lovely features knowing music and dance." And a man whose advertisement

said that he had an American immigration permit was
able to say, "Only girls from rich, well-connected
families need apply."

TURN TO COMPREHENSION CHECK AT END OF CHAPTER

READING TIMES:
1st reading _____ minutes
2nd reading _____ minutes

READING SPEED:
6 minutes = 82 wpm
5 minutes = 98 wpm
4 minutes = 123 wpm
3 minutes = 164 wpm

A. **Analysis of Ideas and Relationships: Circle the letter next to the best answer.**

1. In paragraph 1, sentence 2, "here" refers to:
   a. America.
   b. India.
   c. Sunday.

2. In paragraph 2, who wrote each advertisement—a man or woman? In each case, explain your answer.
   Advertisement 1:   A _____ wrote it.
   Advertisement 2:   A _____ wrote it.
   Advertisement 3:   A _____ wrote it.

3. The main idea of paragraph 3 is that:
   a. India's society is changing.
   b. women work.
   c. arranged marriages are an age-old custom.

4. In paragraph 3, sentence 3:
   a. gives an example of the idea discussed in sentence 2.
   b. is the main idea of the paragraph.
   c. is not related to sentence 2.

5. In paragraph 5, why is "marriage payment" in parentheses?
   a. It explains the meaning of *dowry*.
   b. It isn't as important as *dowry*.
   c. It is illegal.
   Please find another example of this use of parentheses in this article.

6. In paragraph 6, sentence 2, why are the words "such as Brahman and Kshatriya" between commas?
   a. Because Brahman and Kshatriya are unimportant castes.
   b. Because they are examples of various castes.
   c. Because they are two home regions.

7. **Although he does not directly say it**, the Calcutta businessman would probably agree that:
   a. it is a good idea to place marriage advertisements in the newspaper.
   b. it is a bad idea to place marriage advertisements in the newspaper.
   c. it is embarrassing if anyone answers such advertisements.
   Please explain your answer.

8. In paragraph 9, "A person who has one can get what he wants," **one** refers to:
   a. feature.
   b. marriage advertisement.
   c. permit to live abroad.

9. Paragraph 10 gives examples of:
   a. advertisements from two women looking for husbands.
   b. typical marriage advertisements from the Madras newspapers.
   c. the qualities that a person with an immigration permit can ask for— and expect to get.

10. A good title for this article would be:
    a. Why Do People Marry?
    b. Marriage Customs in India Are Changing
    c. Why Indians Read the Sunday Newspapers

B. Interpretation of Words and Phrases: Circle the letter next to the best answer.

1. Millions of Indians **settle down** with a cup of tea and read the newspaper.
   a. relax
   b. get married
   c. agree

2. The bank officer is from a **well-connected family**.
   a. happy family
   b. family with many children
   c. family with good social contacts

3. His salary is **four figures**.
   a. $4,000
   b. between $1,000 and $9,999
   c. four times as much as the average salary

4. This **age-old** custom is changing.
   a. interesting
   b. very old
   c. recent

5. In paragraph 3, "women are still usually described in terms of appearance," **still** means:
   a. quiet.
   b. up to this time.
   c. stop.

6. The women are usually described **in terms of** their appearance.
   a. by publishing
   b. by liking
   c. by considering

7. In paragraph 5, "The fathers of many bridegrooms still require it," **it** refers to:
   a. custom.
   b. marriage payment (dowry).
   c. simple marriage.

8. Divorce is **almost unheard of** in India.
   a. quite unusual
   b. common
   c. deaf

9. "The majority of the advertisements require **not only** caste, **but also** a certain home region and ethnic origin" means that
   a. only a certain caste is required.
   b. only a certain home region and ethnic origin are required.
   c. a certain caste, home region, and ethnic origin are all required.

10. In paragraph 7, "fair" means:
   a. light-skinned.
   b. honest.
   c. average.

   How do you know which meaning of "fair" is correct for paragraph 7?
   a. Tall men usually have a light complexion.
   b. The paragraph is talking about skin color.
   c. The advertisements have many requirements.

C. **Synonyms: From this list, choose a synonym for the word in bold type in each sentence.**

comes toward	especially	special attraction
connections	shows	strong
consider	small	variety
ended		

1. What do you do when a strange dog **approaches** you?

2. I took my girlfriend to see the new **feature** at the movie theater.

3. Of all the coats in that store, I **particularly** like the brown one with the fur collar.

4. An engineer must have a **solid** background in mathematics and science.

5. Mr. Lewis drives a very expensive car and gives lots of big parties. This **reflects** his success in business.

6. The party **broke up** at 1 a.m., and I didn't get home until 2.

7. I have a **slight** cold. I hope it doesn't get worse.

8. I **regard** a good education as being very important to my future.

9. In Mexico, you can always find a wide **range** of fresh fruit in the market.

10. The successful salesman had many **contacts** in several different cities.

D. Prepositions and Verb-Completers: Write any appropriate preposition or verb-completer in the blank spaces.

1. Millions _____ Indians settle down _____ their newspapers, just _____ Americans do.

2. Many people turn _____ the marriage advertisements where they can look _____ husbands and wives.

3. The advertisements reflect the changes _____ the age-old custom _____ the arranged marriage.

4. Are women still described _____ terms _____ their appearance?

5. Divorce used _____ be unheard _____ _____ India.

6. When her marriage broke _____ , she was unhappy.

7. Advertisements are read _____ many people, mostly _____ cities.

8. There's nothing embarrassing _____ placing an advertisement _____ the newspaper.

9. Try _____ do the best you can _____ your family.

10. Because _____ the poor standard _____ living, a permit _____ live abroad is a great attraction.

E. Determiners: Write any appropriate determiner in the blanks below. If no determiner is necessary, write an "X" in the blank. (See Chapter 1 exercise for examples of determiners.)

Advertisements are read by _____ wide range of_____
(1)   (2)
people in _____ upper _____ classes. _____ many
(3)   (4)   (5)
of them receive _____ dozens of _____ answers. "There is
(6)   (7)
_____ nothing embarrassing about it," explained _____
(8)   (9)
Calcutta _____ businessman advertising for _____ son-
(10)   (11)
in-law. "It's just _____ another way of broadening _____
(12)   (13)
contacts and increasing _____ possibilities for _____
(14)   (15)
one's _____ daughter." _____ one of _____ best
(16)   (17)   (18)
attractions _____ advertisement can offer is _____ permit
(19)   (20)
to live abroad, especially in _____ Canada or _____
(21)   (22)
United States.

F. Antonyms: Each sentence contains two opposite words. Circle the word that completes the sentence correctly.

1. Those shirts are usually $15 each, but today they have a (special–regular) price of $9.95.

2. On special holidays, people in my country sing (traditional–modern) songs that were written many years ago.

3. The more people you meet, the more you can (narrow–broaden) your contacts.

4. You will have to (loosen–tighten) the string in order to open the box.

5. The man said, "I am (guilty–innocent). I didn't do it!"

6. The soldier stood in a (relaxed–rigid) position while the general walked past him.

7. That house is so (solid–weak) that it will never fall down.

8. When you (approach–go away from) a friend, you should say "hello."

9. I (usually–rarely) eat dinner in a restaurant because prices are so expensive.

10. Could you help me? This problem is so (simple–complex) that I can't understand it.

G. **Word Forms: Choose the correct word form to fit into each sentence. Use appropriate verb tenses, singular or plural forms for nouns, and passive voice where necessary.**

1. **connection, to connect**
   a. I _____ my tape recorder to the radio and recorded lots of good music.
   b. Is there any _____ between those two families?

2. **preference, to prefer, preferential, preferable, preferably**
   a. What kind of movies do you _____—westerns, dramas, or comedies?
   b. I have no _____ . I like them all.
   c. It is _____ to take children to comedies.
   d. I would _____ to see a drama.
   e. The rich man received _____ treatment in the restaraunt.

3. **increase, to increase, increasing, increasingly**
   a. An _____ number of people are moving into the cities.
   b. It is becoming _____ difficult to find an inexpensive apartment.
   c. The _____ in population is causing housing problems.
   d. The population of my city _____ rapidly these days.

4. **society, to socialize, social, sociable, socially**
   a. In most human _____ , people live together in family groups.
   b. These groups _____ with each other.
   c. This _____ contact is regarded as very important.
   d. Stealing is not _____ acceptable.
   e. The Smiths are very _____ people. They like to give parties very often.

5. **description, to describe, descriptive, indescribable**
   a. A writer must have good _____ abilities.
   b. Can you give me a _____ of the man who broke the window?
   c. The sunset was so beautiful that I can't _____ it.
   d. The sunset was so beautiful that it is _____ .

6. **appearance, to appear, apparent, apparently**
   a. Mr. Ivanov _____ to be very tired today.
   b. _____ , he didn't sleep well last night.
   c. It is _____ that he didn't sleep well.
   d. He gives the _____ of being very tired.

7. **explanation, to explain, explanatory**
   a. I don't understand the question. Could you please _____ it?
   b. His _____ of the problem was very clear.
   c. Some books have _____ notes at the bottom of the page.

8. **width, to widen, wide, widely**
   a. The city wants _____ the street in front of my house.
   b. The _____ of the street will be increased by 12 feet (4 meters).
   c. If they make the street too _____ , there will be lots of traffic here.
   d. The people in my neighborhood have _____ differing opinions on the need for a bigger street.

9. **possibility, possible, impossible, possibly**
   a. Could you _____ come at 11 o'clock instead of at 10?
   b. I'm sorry. That would be_____ .
   c. However, it is _____ for me to come at noon.
   d. Yes, that's a good _____ for me too.

10. **attraction, to attract, attractive, attractively**
    a. Mrs. Rojas always dresses very _____ .
    b. The loud noise _____ everyone in the neighborhood.
    c. I went to see that movie because the advertisements were so _____ .
    d. The circus is always a big _____ for children.

H. Sentence Scramble: Make a sentence out of each group of words.

1. settle down – millions – their – with – of Indians – weekend newspapers

2. look for – husbands and wives – in – the – advertisements – marriage – young people

3. are – described – appearance – women – still – in terms of

4. advertisements – by – range – of people – are read – a – eagerly – wide

5. who – immigration permit – has – person – an – a – what he wants – get – can

I. Topics for Discussion and Composition:

1. This article describes an accepted way of finding a husband or wife in India. What is your reaction to this article? Do you think that newspaper advertisements are a good way to find a husband or wife? Why or why not? Please explain your answer.

2. How do young people in your country find a husband or wife? Is this similar to or different from the Indian custom? How important is the parents' decision in a marriage in your country? Give some examples to explain your answer.

3. This article described some of the features that Indians consider important in a husband or wife. What do people in your country think is important when they are looking for a husband or wife? Why do they think so? (Examples: appearance, skills, earning power, love, etc.)

4. What are the traditional ideas about marriage in your country? Are these traditional ideas changing? Or have they remained the same? Are social changes causing any of the changes in marriage customs? Please explain your answer.

5. This article says that the attitude toward divorce is changing in India. What is the attitude toward divorce in your country? Is this a traditional view? Is the traditional view changing? Please give some examples.

6. Pretend that you live in India. Write a marriage advertisement for yourself. Be sure to include some description of yourself as well as the requirements for your husband/wife. Then, write an explanation of why you want a person with these requirements.

J. **Reading Reconstruction: Read this paragraph as many times as you can in three minutes. Then, with your book closed, try to restate the ideas as clearly and completely as you can. (See Chapter 1 exercise for complete instructions.)**

Marriage in the United States

In the United States, young men and women prefer to find their own husbands and wives. This reflects many of the customs of American society. Men and women go to school together and work together, so they come into contact with a wide range of people. They are attracted to a certain person for many reasons, but "love" is regarded as particularly important in their choice. Americans often explain their reason for getting married by saying, "I love him/I love her."

Key words (to be put on the chalkboard):

prefer	contact	regarded
reflects	wide	particularly
customs	range	explain
society	attracted	

K. Comprehension Check: On a separate piece of paper, write the numbers 1 through 10 on both sides. Mark one side "Test 1" and the other side "Test 2." Read each statement and decide whether it is true or false. Write "T" after true statements and "F" after false statements under Test 1. After you have finished the comprehension check, turn Test 1 face down. Then read the article again and do the comprehension check again under Test 2. Base your answers on the information in this article *only*, even if you disagree with what the author said.

1. Many people read marriage advertisements in India.

2. According to this article, there is a special season when people in India marry.

3. Customs in India are changing.

4. There are very few marriage advertisements in the newspapers.

5. Women in India never work.

6. Indians never get divorced.

7. Some families still require a dowry (marriage payment).

8. Most of the people who read the advertisements are in the upper classes and want to broaden their contacts.

9. People in India are embarrassed by the advertisements.

10. A man with an immigration permit can find a good wife easily.

8

EXPLODING THE MYTHS ABOUT THE AMERICAN FAMILY

[Dr. Mary Jo Bane is the associate director of the Center for Research on Women and a professor of education at Wellesley College. Dr. Bane is interested in the American family and how it is changing. The results of her research are published in a book entitled *Here to Stay: American Families in the Twentieth Century.*]

1   *The American family is dying. The highest divorce rate in history indicates that marriage is becoming unpopular. Most young people today have no intention of marrying and raising a family. More and more working women abandon their children to baby-sitters or day-care centers.*

2   What you've just read sounds true, doesn't it? But it's all false. A new study reveals that the American family is stronger than ever. This study, conducted by Dr. Mary Joe Bane, analyzes past and **current** census data and other sociological research about the American family.

present

3   Dr. Bane says, "I started my research with the idea that the American family was **going to hell** and needed to be replaced by some new child-care institutions. I wanted to prove this with statistics. I believed all the **myths**, but statistics showed that the American family wasn't dying." Instead, Dr. Bane found "surprising evidence of the **persistence** of American commitments to family life." What's needed—rather than the speeches about the problems of the family—is a more accurate diagnosis of the family's current condition, according to Dr. Bane.

failing

false beliefs

strength

destroy

argue against

rapidly grow-
ing

4   Dr. Bane's study and several others **shatter** many of the myths about the American family. Let's take a look at some of the myths—and the facts that **refute** them.

5   Myth 1:   THE AMERICAN FAMILY IS DY-ING BECAUSE OF THE **SOARING** DIVORCE RATE.

The American family is changing, not dying: It is becoming smaller, women are becoming more equal, and the divorce rate is high. But Dr. Bane says that, despite the high divorce rate, "marriage has never been more popular. The majority of divorced people re-marry, but only 2% marry more than twice. In the

without sub-
stance

United States, most marriages are not **fly-by-night**, and people don't continually change partners without marriage. Most marriages last a long time, and a large proportion of divorces are from teenage marriages. Depending on the specific situation, there's often good reason for teenage marriages to break up."

destroying/
not taking
care of

6   Myth   2:   WORKING   MOTHERS   ARE **WRECKING** THE FAMILY BY **NEGLECTING** THEIR CHILDREN.

"There's no evidence that children receive less attention from mothers who work outside the home than from mothers working inside the home," says Dr. Bane. "You have to divide the time into different cate-gories: simple physical and custodial functions, and educational time or development time when a mother plays with the child. So far we haven't seen the amount

change

of educational or development time **vary** much, whether or not the mother works outside the home."

make up for

7   In fact, Dr. Bane finds evidence that working mothers—especially in the middle class—try to **compensate for** working by setting aside time exclu-sively for their children. "They probably read more to their children and spend more time in planned activi-ties with them than nonworking mothers do," says Dr. Bane.

8   In her book, *Here to Stay: American Families in the Twentieth Century,* Dr. Bane says, "Television—not working mothers—is by far the most significant new child-care arrangement of this century. The most important activity for children up to age 14 is watching television. The average preschooler watches TV about 33 hours a week, one-third of his waking hours. The average sixth grader watches about 31 hours of television a week."

9   School is the second most time-consuming activity for children. They spend an average of about 19 hours a week in school. A larger proportion of children go to school now than ever before, and they stay in school longer. Another big change is the proportion of very young children enrolled in nursery schools and kindergartens: from 27% in 1965 to 41% in 1973. Compared with these two dramatic changes in child activity—greater hours devoted to television and to school—the changes caused by mothers working outside the home "appear almost **trivial**, according to Dr.   **unimportant** Bane.

TURN TO COMPREHENSION CHECK AT END OF CHAPTER

READING TIMES:
1st reading _____ minutes
2nd reading_____ minutes

READING SPEED:
8 minutes = 110 wpm
7 minutes = 126 wpm
6 minutes = 147 wpm
5 minutes = 176 wpm
4 minutes = 220 wpm

A. Analysis of Ideas and Relationships: Circle the letter next to the best answer.

1. The main idea of this article is that:
   a. the American family is dying.
   b. young people today don't want to get married.
   c. the American family is changing, but it is stronger than ever.

2. How did Dr. Bane feel about the results of her study?
   a. She was surprised.
   b. She was disappointed.
   c. She was not surprised.

   Why do you think so?

3. Which statement is *not* true?
   a. The American family is becoming smaller.
   b. The divorce rate is going down.
   c. American women are becoming more equal.

4. Paragraph 5:
   a. gives examples of today's marriage patterns.
   b. explains how divorce is destroying the family.
   c. suggests that marriage is becoming unpopular.

5. It is true that:
   a. there is no evidence that children receive less attention from mothers who work outside the home.
   b. working mothers neglect their children.
   c. working mothers don't spend as much educational or developmental time with their children.

6. What is the most significant new child-care arrangement of this century?
   a. Day-care centers.
   b. Television.
   c. Babysitters who are not members of the family.

7. Put the following statements into logical order. Then refer to paragraph 8 to check your work.
   a. "The average preschooler watches TV about 33 hours a week, one-third of his waking hours."
   b. "The most important activity for children up to age 14 is watching television."
   c. "Television—not working mothers—is by far the most significant new child-care arrangement of this century."

8. After television, what is the second most significant activity for children now?
   a. School.
   b. Sports.
   c. Religious activities.

9. Which statement is true?
   a. The proportion of very young children attending nursery schools and kindergartens is decreasing.
   b. The proportion of very young children attending nursery schools and kindergartens is increasing.
   c. The proportion of very young children attending nursery schools and kindergartens is staying the same.

10. Dr. Bane believes that:
    a. the American family is here to stay.
    b. children should not watch so much television.
    c. mothers should not work when their children are small.

B. Interpretation of Words and Phrases: Circle the letter next to the best answer.

1. "I started my research with the idea that the American family was **going to hell.**"
   a. sinful
   b. failing
   c. succeeding

2. "I believed all the **myths** about the American family." In this context, **myths** means
   a. false beliefs.
   b. ancient legends.
   c. stories about gods and goddesses.

3. Dr. Bane's study **shatters** many of the myths about the American family.
   a. splits
   b. destroys
   c. breaks into tiny pieces

4. Let's **take a look at** some of the myths.
   a. examine
   b. stare at
   c. glance at

5. Working mothers **set aside** time for their children.
   a. don't allow
   b. reserve
   c. forget about

6. Working mothers try to **compensate for** working by spending a certain amount of time in planned activities with their children.
   a. pay for
   b. forget about
   c. make up for

7. "Television—not working mothers—is **by far** the most significant new child-care arrangement of this century."
   a. far away
   b. perhaps
   c. definitely

8. "The most important activity for children **up to** age 14 is watching television."
   a. after
   b. until
   c. at

9. "They spend an average of about 19 hours a week in school." This means that:
   a. everybody spends 19 hours a week in school.
   b. some people spend more than 19 hours a week in school.
   c. some people spend more than 19 hours a week in school, and some people spend less than 19 hours a week in school.

10. Dr. Bane believes that the American family is **here to stay.**
    a. going to survive
    b. not changing
    c. not going anywhere

C. Synonyms: From this list, choose a synonym for the word in bold type in each sentence.

keep on trying	takes a lot of time
mean	an insubstantial and undependable
up-to-date	easy to do
doesn't take care of	not true
argue against	destroyed

1. He decided not to invest any money in that restaurant because it looked like **a fly-by-night** operation.

2. If you want to succeed in anything, you must **be persistent.**

3. She **neglects** her children.

4. Can you **refute** that statement?

5. These figures are not **current.**

6. At first I thought that math problem was going to be difficult, but it turned out to be **trivial.**

7. Is this statement true or **false?**

8. Their car was **completely wrecked** in that accident.

9. I am sorry; I didn't **intend** to hurt your feelings.

10. This activity **is very time-consuming.**

D. Prepositions and Verb-Completers: Write any appropriate preposition or verb-completer in the blank spaces.

1. Dr. Bane is interested _____ the American family.

2. According _____ Dr. Bane, many _____ the ideas people have _____ the American family are false.

3. Dr. Bane found surprising evidence _____ American commitments _____ family life.

4. Let's take a look _____ some _____ the myths—and the facts that refute them.

5. It is not true that the American family is dying because _____ the soaring divorce rate.

6. _____ the United States, most marriages last a long time.

7. A large proportion _____ divorces are _____ teenage marriages.

8. Depending_____ the specific situation, there's often good reason _____ teenage marriages _____ break _____ .

9. It is also not true that children receive less attention _____ mothers who work outside the home than _____ mothers working inside the home.

10. _____ far the most significant new child-care arrangement _____ this century is television.

E. Cloze Exercise: Fill in the blanks with any appropriate word.

"There's no evidence that _____ receive less attention from
                                        (1)
_____ who work outside the _____ than from mothers
        (2)   (3)
working _____ the home," says Dr. Bane. " _____ have to
              (4)   (5)
divide the _____ into different categories: simple _____
                  (6)   (7)
and custodial functions, and _____ time or development time
                                          (8)
_____ a mother plays with _____ child."
        (9)   (10)

F. Punctuation Exercise: Write in capital letters, periods, and commas where needed.

in her book *here to stay: american families in the twentieth century* dr bane says "television—not working mothers—is by far the most significant new child-care arrangement of this century the most important activity for children up to age 14 is watching television the average preschooler watches tv about 33 hours a week one-third of his waking hours the average sixth grader watches about 31 hours of television a week

G. **Word Forms: Choose the correct word form to fit into each sentence. Use appropriate verb tenses, singular or plural forms for nouns, and passive voice where necessary.**

1. **indicator, indication, to indicate, indicative**
   a. Was there any _____ that something was wrong?
   b. The gasoline _____ showed that the tank was almost empty.
   c. Would you please read my paper and _____ in the margin wherever you think I ought to make changes?
   d. The price of that diamond is _____ of its quality.

2. **change, to change, changing, changed**
   a. Thank goodness, the wind seems to be _____ .
   b. It is hard to _____ .
   c. He was a _____ man after that experience.
   d. I noticed a _____ in his behavior.

3. **revelation, to reveal, revealing, revealingly**
   a. I never knew anything about that; this comes as a _____ to me.
   b. She gave him a _____ look.
   c. She looked at him _____ .
   d. He never _____ what they had discussed.

4. **analysis, to analyze, analytical, analytically**
   a. Can you _____ this problem?
   b. She has an _____ mind.
   c. Tell me your _____ of the situation in the Middle East.
   d. Look at the situation _____ .

5. **sociologist, sociology, sociological**
   a. I think you might enjoy taking a _____ course.
   b. What is the _____ importance of this study?
   c. She is a famous _____ .

6. **commitment, to commit**
   a. Did you ever _____ an act that you regretted later?
   b. You have to give me a _____ that you will do your best on the project.

7. **diagnosis, to diagnose, diagnostic**
   a. Unfortunately, the _____ was cancer.
   b. How did you _____ it?
   c. We used _____ tests.

8. **developer, development, to develop**
   a. Are there any new _____ in the case?
   b. He is a famous real estate _____ .
   c. We _____ a plan and presented it to the board.

9. **dramatist, dramatics, drama, to dramatize, dramatic, dramatically**
   a. She always dressed very _____ .
   b. He was a famous 19th century _____ .
   c. They are studying in the _____ department.
   d. The ending of the book is very _____ .
   e. Try to _____ the idea.

10. **care, to care, careful, carefully**
    a. I don't _____ what you say; I'm going to do it.
    b. Please be _____ when you're driving.
    c. Watch the road _____ .
    d. They give the patients a lot of _____ in the hospital.

H. **Sentence Scramble: Make a sentence out of each group of words.**

1. changing – American – the – family – is

2. marriage – never – popular – than – more – has – been – it – is – today

3. true – divorce – it – is – that – the – rate – high – is

4. however – long – time – last – most – marriages – a

5. remarry – people – divorced – of – majority – the

I. Topics for Discussion and Composition:

1. Divorce rates are rapidly increasing in most countries around the world and, consequently, families are changing. Children are obviously very much affected by the divorce of their parents. How do you think parents should handle divorce? What could society do to help the children—and the parents—through divorce? Please give several suggestions and specific examples to illustrate these suggestions.

2. The world would be better off if children never watched television. Do you agree or disagree? Why? Please give reasons for your answer and give specific examples to illustrate your reasons.

3. Many people think that television is partially responsible for the increase in violence in society. Other people disagree, and they blame the increase in violence on other factors. Do you think television and violence in society are connected? Why? Or why not? Please give several reasons for your answer and give specific examples to illustrate your reasons.

4. "Working mothers are wrecking the family by neglecting their children." Dr. Bane disagrees with this statement, and she states that "there's no evidence that children receive less attention from mothers who work outside the home than from mothers working inside the home." What do you think? Why? Be as specific as possible. Please give examples from your experience or from the experience of others.

5. Society should make it more difficult for people to get married. Too many people jump into marriage without understanding what they are getting into. Do you agree or disagree? Why? Can society do anything to make people more aware of the responsibilities of marriage? *Should* society do anything to make people more aware of these responsibilities? Please be specific and give examples.

6. Divorce is not necessarily evil. Do you agree or disagree? Why? Please give reasons and specific examples to support your point of view.

J. Reading Reconstruction: Read this paragraph as many times as you can in three minutes. Then, with your book closed, try to restate the ideas as clearly and completely as you can. (See Chapter 1 exercise for complete instructions.)

Working Mothers in the U.S.A.

The majority of American women with children now work outside the home. Society has been slow to accept this fact, and it has done little to make life easier for working mothers. Good, reliable child care is a problem. There are not enough day-care centers, and many working mothers do not have mothers or aunts or sisters who are available to help them take care of the children. It is true that fathers do more to help with the children than they did in the past. But they too have jobs and other responsibilities that prevent them from helping more. Working mothers are not satisfied with the child-care arrangements available to them. But what can they do? Where can they turn? These are critical questions for working mothers.

Key words (to be written on the chalkboard):

working mothers	available	satisfied
majority	take care	arrangements
society	responsibilities	critical
reliable	prevent	questions
child care		

K. Comprehension Check: On a separate piece of paper, write the numbers 1 through 10 on both sides. Mark one side "Test 1" and the other side "Test 2." Read each statement and decide whether it is true or false. Write "T" after true statements and "F" after false statements under Test 1. After you have finished the comprehension check, turn Test 1 face down. Then read the article again and do the comprehension check again under Test 2. Base your answers on the information in this article *only,* even if you disagree with what the author said.

1. It is a myth that the American family is dying.

2. Dr. Bane said that, before she started her research, she believed that the American family was failing.

3. Her study showed that the American family is stronger than ever.

4. The American family is becoming smaller.

5. The divorce rate is decreasing.

6. Most divorced people remarry.

7. Most marriages last a long time.

8. Working mothers do not give enough time and attention to their children, according to Dr. Bane.

9. Television is the most significant new child-care arrangement of the 20th century.

10. This article says that television is bad for children.

Review Examination II (Chapters 5, 6, 7, 8)

A. Prepositions and Verb-Completers: Write any appropriate preposition or verb-completer in the blank spaces. (20 points: 1 point each.)

1. Nutrition depends _____ what types _____ food you eat.

2. You have _____ eat fewer calories _____ order _____ lose weight.

3. Advertisements are read _____ many people, mostly _____ cities.

4. Divorce used _____ be unheard _____ _____ India.

5. More comic books are read _____ Mexico than _____ any other Latin American country.

6. There's nothing wrong _____ comic books; it's just a question _____ how they are used.

7. According _____ Dr. Bane, many _____ the ideas people have _____ the American family are false.

8. Dr. Bane found surprising evidence _____ American commitments _____ family life.

9. Dr. Bane is interested _____ the American family.

B. Word Forms: Look at the first word in each line. Write the appropriate form of this word in the sentence that follows it. Be careful to use appropriate verb tenses, singular and plural forms for nouns, and passive voice where necessary. (50 points: 2 points each.)

(Example)

evidence: It is ____*evident*____ that you studied.

1. **know:** He spoke very _____ about French history.

2. **information:** They _____ you when it is time to leave.

3. **valuable:** What is the _____ of that painting?

4. **freshness:** I would like some _____ fruit for dessert.

5. **break:** It _____ my heart when my dog died.

6. **nature:** Can animals live _____ in a zoo?

7. **prefer:** My _____ is to play golf.

8. **increase:** An _____ large number of people are jogging.

9. **apparent:** Mrs. Ito _____ very happy today.

10. **socialize:** In Indian _____ , marriage is very important.

11. **possibility:** It wasn't _____ to visit her.

12. **attract:** That's a very _____ coat you're wearing.

13. **explanation:** I _____ it to you tomorrow.

14. **hide:** She kept her illness _____ from everyone.

15. **physical:** That is such _____ hard work.

16. **compete:** A French pianist won the _____ .

17. **adoption:** I _____ a skinny cat that I found on the street.

18. **total:** You are _____ right about that.

19. **defensive:** Let me speak in my own _____ .

20. **indication:** This test _____ that you are very smart.

21. **change:** He's very creative. His ideas are always _____ .

22. **analytical:** The doctor made an _____ of my blood.

23. **commit:** She has a great _____ to art.

24. **drama:** Why must you always speak so _____ ?

25. **care:** Who _____ for your plants while you are on vacation?

C. Synonyms: From this list, choose a synonym for the word in bold type in the sentences below. (20 points: 2 points each.)

connections	get along with	strong
consider	keep on trying	up-to-date
exactly the same	sees no difference	very popular
for each person		

1. Your body **makes no distinction** between natural and synthetic vitamins.

2. Those twin girls look **identical.**

3. That house is so **solid** it will never fall down.

4. I **regard** French cooking as the best.

5. Marriage advertisements broaden our **contacts.**

6. The Beatles made many **hit** records.

7. How do you **deal with** a noisy neighbor?

8. How many televisions are there **per capita** in your country?

9. If you **are persistent**, you will succeed.

10. She always dresses in the most **current** fashions.

D. Determiners: Write any appropriate determiner in the blanks. If no determiner is necessary, write an "X" in the blank. (10 points: 1 point each.)

Every _____ Sunday morning, _____ millions of
       (1)   (2)
Indians settle down with _____ cup of _____ coffee and
                               (3)   (4)
_____ weekend issues of _____ newspapers, just as
     (5)   (6)
_____ Americans do. But here, with _____ marriage
     (7)   (8)
season approaching, _____ many of them turn quickly to
                          (9)
_____ Sunday feature that is particularly Indian.
     (10)

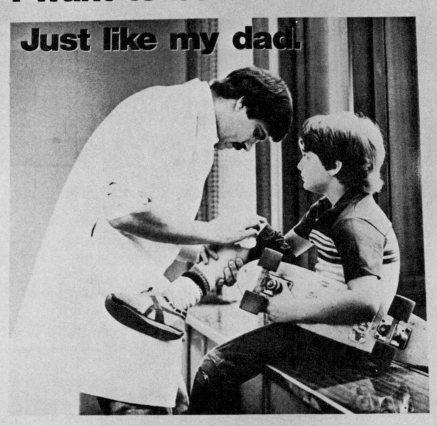

When I grow up, I want to be a nurse.

Just like my dad.

Nursing: A career for women and men.

9

WOMEN'S WORK?

[Beginning in the 1960s, American women started entering jobs and professions that had been dominated almost completely by men. In the 1970s, another pattern emerged in employment: men began entering jobs and professions previously dominated by women. This article looks at some of the professions men have recently entered. It examines the reasons behind these career choices, and it also mentions some of the changes men are making in "women's work."]

1   When Donald Olayer enrolled in nursing school nine years ago, his father **took it hard**. "Here's my father, a steelworker, hearing about other steelworkers' sons who were becoming welders or getting football scholarships," Mr. Olayer recalls. "The thought of his son becoming a nurse was too much."

was upset

2   Today, Mr. Olayer, a registered nurse trained as an anesthetist, earns about $30,000 a year at Jameson Memorial Hospital in New Castle, Pennsylvania. His father, he says, has "**done an about face**. Now he tells the guys he works with that their sons, who can't find jobs even after four years of college, should have become nurses."

completely changed

3   That's not an unusual **turnabout** nowadays. Just as women have **gained a footing in** nearly every occupation once reserved for men, men can be found today working routinely in a wide variety of jobs once held nearly **exclusively** by women. The men are working as receptionists and flight attendants, servants, and even "**Kelly girls**."

complete change/entered into

entirely

temporary office workers

4   The Urban Institute, a research group in Washington, recently estimated that the number of male secretaries rose 24% to 31,000 in 1978 from 25,000 in

time period

1972. The number of male telephone operators over the same **span** rose 38%, and the number of male nurses 94%. Labor experts expect the trend to continue.

stated

Job Availability *Cited*

5   For one thing, tightness in the job market seems to have given men an additional incentive to take jobs where they can find them. Although female-dominated office and service jobs for the most part rank lower in

they're available

pay and status, "**they're still there**," says June O'Neill, director of program and policy research at the institute.

physical labor

Traditionally male **blue-collar** jobs, meanwhile, "aren't increasing at all."

viewpoints

6   At the same time, she says, "The **outlooks** of young people are different." Younger men with less rigid views on what constitutes male or female work

social disapproval

"may not feel there's such a **stigma** to working in a female-dominated field."

separation

7   Although views have softened, men who cross the sexual **segregation** line in the job market may still face discrimination and ridicule. David Anderson, a 36-year-old former high school teacher, says he found secretarial work "a way out of teaching and into the business world." He had applied for work at 23 employment agencies for "management training jobs that didn't exist," and he discovered that "the best skill I had was being able to type 70 words a minute."

8   He took a job as a secretary to the marketing director of a New York publishing company. But he says he could feel a lot of people wondering what I was doing there and if something was wrong with me."

bring

9   Mr. Anderson's boss was a woman. When she asked him to **fetch** coffee, he says, "the other secretaries' eyebrows went up. Sales executives who came in to see his boss, he says, "couldn't quite believe that I could and would type, take dictation, and answer the phones."

10   Males sometimes find themselves mistaken for higher-status professionals. Anthony Shee, a flight attendant with US Air Inc., has been mistaken for a pilot. Mr. Anderson, the secretary, says he found himself being "treated **in executive tones** whenever I wore a suit."

as an executive

11   In fact, the men in traditional female jobs often **move up the ladder fast**. Mr. Anderson actually worked only seven months as a secretary. Then he got a higher-level, better-paying job as a placement counselor at an employment agency. "I got a lot of encouragement to advance," he says, including job **tips** from male executives who couldn't quite see me staying a secretary."

advance quickly

information

12   Experts say, for example, that while men make up only a small fraction of elementary school teachers, a disproportionate number of elementary principals are men. Barbara Bergmann, an economist at the University of Maryland who has studied sex segregation at work, believes that's partly because of "sexism in the occupational structure" and partly because men have been raised to assert themselves and to assume responsibility. Men may also feel more compelled than women to advance, she suspects.

Moving Up

13   Donald Olayer, the nurse, is typical. Almost as soon as he graduated from nursing school, he says he decided "not to stay just a regular floor nurse earning only $12,000 a year." Now he can look forward to earning three times that much, "enough to support a family on," he says, and he also has "much more responsibility."

14   Men are more likely than women to see nursing as a full-time career, Mr. Olayer says. He also says the men are more assertive. "Men don't **buy** the Florence Nightingale garbage they teach in nursing school— that the doctor is everything, and the nurse is there just to take orders," he says. "Men will ask questions more and think for themselves."

accept

15   But in asserting themselves, the males in female-dominated fields may be making life easier for the women, too. "Guys get together and organize and are willing to fight for more," Mr. Olayer says. "Once we get a 30% to 40% ratio of men in nursing, you'll see salaries and the whole status of the job improve."

TURN TO COMPREHENSION CHECK AT END OF CHAPTER

READING TIMES:
1st reading _____ minutes
2nd reading_____ minutes

READING SPEED:
10 minutes = 108 wpm
9 minutes = 120 wpm
8 minutes = 135 wpm
7 minutes = 155 wpm
5 minutes = 216 wpm

A. Analysis of Ideas and Relationships: Circle the letter next to the best answer.

1. This article is about:
   a. men entering into professions that have been dominated by women.
   b. women entering into professions that have been dominated by men.
   c. the advantages of entering the field of nursing.

2. Read paragraphs 1 and 2 again. Mr. Olayer's father changed his mind about his son being a nurse because:
   a. he learned more about the nursing field.
   b. his son has a job with a good salary at a time when many highly qualified people cannot find work.
   c. most of the people in the nursing field are now men (unlike nine years ago when Donald Olayer first enrolled in nursing school).

3. Paragraph 3 explains that:
   a. Donald Olayer's story is typical of many men today who are working in jobs once held almost exclusively by women.
   b. Donald Olayer's story is quite unusual because men have not entered women-dominated fields to any great extent.
   c. Donald Olayer thinks now that he made a big mistake when he entered the field of nursing.

4. Which statement is NOT true?
   a. Men have taken jobs in female-dominated careers because these jobs were available.
   b. Physical labor (blue-collar) jobs were not increasing.
   c. Men have taken jobs in female-dominated careers because these jobs pay more.

5. Paragraph 6 suggests that:
   a. young people have more rigid ideas about male or female work than their parents do.
   b. young people have less rigid ideas about male or female work than their parents do.
   c. parents have less rigid ideas about male or female work than their children do.

6. David Anderson says:
   a. he encountered some discrimination and ridicule when he was working as a secretary.
   b. he received encouragement and acceptance from the women secretaries.
   c. men make better secretaries than women do.

7. Why was Anthony Shee, a flight attendant with US Air Inc., mistaken for a pilot?
   a. Because he always wore a pilot's uniform.
   b. Because he told people he was a pilot instead of a flight attendant.
   c. Because men in women-dominated fields sometimes find themselves mistaken for higher-status professionals.

8. Which statement is NOT true?
   a. Women are more assertive than men at work.
   b. Men are more assertive than women at work.
   c. Men have traditionally been raised to assume more responsibility than women have.

9. Men may:
   a. feel the need to advance at work more than women do.
   b. be smarter than women are.
   c. be better employees than women are.

10. Men in female-dominated fields may:
   a. be taking jobs away from women.
   b. be making life easier for women in their fields.
   c. be better qualified than women are.

B. **Interpretation of Words and Phrases: Circle the letter next to the best answer.**

1. "When Donald Olayer enrolled in nursing school nine years ago, his father **took it hard**."
   a. was disappointed and upset
   b. was excited and happy
   c. was indifferent

2. "The thought of his son becoming a nurse was **too much**."
   a. overwhelming and unacceptable
   b. completely unexpected
   c. delightful

3. "His father has **done an about face**."
   a. turned around
   b. completely changed his mind
   c. turned his face around

4. "Now he tells the **guys** he works with that their sons should have become nurses."
   a. women
   b. children
   c. men

5. "That's not an unusual **turnabout** nowadays."
   a. change of position
   b. movement
   c. turn

6. "Women have gained a footing in nearly every occupation once reserved for men."
    a. Women now outnumber men in occupations once reserved exclusively for men.
    b. Women are now well represented in occupations once reserved exclusively for men.
    c. Women are not allowed in occupations reserved for men.

7. "The other secretaries' eyebrows went up" means:
    a. the other secretaries were surprised by his action (when he brought coffee for his boss).
    b. the other secretaries stared at him.
    c. the other secretaries wore a lot of eye makeup.

8. Mr. Anderson says he found himself being treated **in executive tones** whenever he wore a suit.
    a. in quiet, neutral colors
    b. as if he were an executive
    c. with a lack of respect

9. "Men in traditional female jobs often **move up the ladder fast**."
    a. work upstairs
    b. climb stairs quickly
    c. advance quickly at work

10. "Men don't buy the Florence Nightingale garbage they teach in nursing school—that the doctor is everything, and the nurse is there just to take orders."
    a. Men nurses believe that nurses are more important than doctors and doctors should take orders from nurses without asking any questions.
    b. Men nurses believe that doctors should have more authority and power and nurses should take orders without asking any questions.
    c. Men nurses don't accept the traditional status difference between doctors and nurses where nurses were trained to take orders from doctors without question; men nurses believe that nurses should be more assertive and ask questions.

C. **Synonyms: From this list, choose a synonym for the word in bold type in each sentence.**

makes up	take on	outspoken
increased	viewpoints	expect
unbending	social disapproval	prestige
state		

1. Young people have different **outlooks** today.

2. Their ideas about occupations for men and women are not as **rigid** as older people's ideas are.

3. The **stigma** attached to men working in female-dominated fields is not as great as it used to be.

4. Men nurses tend to be more **assertive** than women nurses do.

5. Men have always been encouraged to **assume** responsibility.

6. The number of male secretaries **rose** from 25,000 in 1972 to 31,000 in 1978.

7. Female-dominated office and service jobs for the most part rank lower in pay and **status**.

8. The Urban Institute studies **cite** a number of reasons why men have entered female-dominated fields.

9. It is no longer clear what **constitutes** male or female work.

10. Women can **look forward to** higher salaries as more men enter female-dominated fields.

D. **Prepositions and Verb-Completers: Write any appropriate preposition or verb-completer in the blank spaces.**

1. When Donald Olayer enrolled _____ nursing school nine years ago, his father was upset and disappointed.

2. The thought _____ his son becoming a nurse was too much.

3. Men are now working _____ a wide variety _____ jobs once held nearly exclusively _____ women.

4. The number _____ male secretaries increased _____ 25,000 _____ 1972 _____ 31,000 _____ 1978.

5. Female-dominated office and service jobs _____ the most part rank lower _____ pay and status.

6. One _____ the main reasons men have gone _____ female-dominated fields is that jobs are available _____ these fields.

7. Men tend _____ be more assertive _____ work.

8. Men get a lot _____ encouragement _____ advance including job tips _____ male executives.

9. The males _____ female-dominated fields may be making life easier _____ the women, too.

10. Once there is a 30% _____ 40% ratio _____ men _____ nursing, salaries and the whole status _____ the job will improve.

E. Cloze Exercise: Fill in the blanks with any appropriate word.

When Donald Olayer enrolled _____ nursing school nine
(1)
years _____ , his father took it _____ . "Here's my father, a
(2)   (3)
steelworker, _____ about other steelworkers' sons _____
(4)   (5)
were becoming welders or _____ football scholarships," Mr.
(6)
Olayer _____ . "The thought of his _____ becoming a
(7)   (8)
nurse was _____ much."
(9)

Today, Mr. Olayer, _____ registered nurse trained as
(10)
_____ anesthetist, earns about $30,000 _____ year at
(11)   (12)
Jameson Memorial Hospital _____ New Castle, Pennsylvania.
(13)

F. Punctuation Exercise: Write in capital letters, periods, and commas where needed.

just as women have gained a footing in nearly every occupation once reserved for men men can be found today working routinely in a wide variety of jobs once held nearly exclusively by women the men are working as receptionists and flight attendants servants and even "kelly girls" the urban institute a research group in washington recently estimated that the number of male secretaries rose 24% to 31000 in 1978 from 25000 in 1972 the number of male telephone operators over the same span rose 38% and the number of male nurses 94% labor experts expect the trend to continue

G. Word Forms: Choose the correct word form to fit into each sentence. Use appropriate verb tenses, singular or plural forms for nouns, and passive voice where necessary.

1. **enrollment, to enroll**
   a. Try to _____ early for that class.
   b. The _____ of my school is going up.

2. **trainer, trainee, training, to train**
   a. He _____ as a nurse five years ago.
   b. You will receive excellent _____ in that school.
   c. She was a horse _____ .
   d. You can start out in a management_____ program, which lasts about six months.

3. **flight, to fly, flight (flying)**
   a. How long is the _____ time between San Francisco and Honolulu?
   b. Which _____ will you be on?
   c. He never liked to _____ at night.

4. **operator, operation, to operate, operating**
   a. Have you ever had an _____ ?
   b. Where is the _____ room?
   c. He is working as a telephone _____ .
   d. The doctors _____ immediately.

5. **tradition, traditional, traditionally**
   a. I am interested in the _____ of other cultures.
   b. _____ , there have been many more women than men in the field of nursing.
   c. She wore a _____ wedding dress.

6. **segregation, to segregate, segregated**
   a. Racial _____ is, unfortunately, still a factor.
   b. They attended a _____ school.
   c. Could you please _____ these buttons by size?

7. **discrimination, to discriminate**
   a. Can you _____ between these two shades of blue?
   b. He faced _____ and ridicule when he first started working as a secretary.

8. **ridicule, to ridicule, ridiculous, ridiculously**
   a. The instruction handbook was _____ complicated.
   b. No one enjoys being the object of _____ .
   c. The children _____ by the other children because of their last name.
   d. This situation is _____ .

9. **employer, employee, employment, to employ**
   a. I _____ at the same place for more than 12 years now.
   b. Where is your place of _____ ?
   c. It takes time for new _____ to learn the procedures in that department.
   d. My _____ gave me a very generous bonus at the end of the year.

10. **encouragement, to encourage, encouraging, encouragingly**
   a. It is wonderful to receive words of _____ .
   b. Thank you for your _____ words.
   c. Her parents _____ her to succeed.
   d. They smiled at her _____ .

H. Sentence Scramble: Make a sentence out of each group of words.

1. new – men – enter – beginning – to – are – fields

2. available – female-dominated – more – jobs – are – fields – in

3. assertive – tend – be – to – men – more

4. rigid – less – ideas – people – younger – usually – have – parents – their – do – than

5. men – advance – more – than – women – quickly – do – work – at

I. Topics for Discussion and Composition:

1. Many people believe that certain types of jobs are men's jobs and others are women's jobs. Do you believe in distinctions between men's and women's jobs? Why? Or why not? Please give several reasons to explain your position and give specific examples to illustrate your reasons.

2. The most important element in job satisfaction is money. Do you agree or disagree? Why? Please give several reasons for your position and specific examples to illustrate your reasons.

3. The most important role of schools is to prepare people for jobs. Do you agree or disagree? Please give several reasons for your position and illustrate these reasons with specific examples from your own experience or the experience of others.

4. Men make better doctors, and women make better nurses. Do you agree or disagree? Please give several reasons for your position and illustrate these reasons with specific examples from your own experience or the experience of others.

5. Please describe the kind of job you would like to have someday. Why would you like to have this job? What are the most important elements of job satisfaction for you?

6. Do you think an adult can be healthy and happy without working? Why? Or why not? Please give several reasons for your position and illustrate these reasons with specific examples from your own experience or the experience of others.

7. How important are personal relationships at work? Please describe productive employer-employee relationships and employee-employee relationships. What are your feelings about the people you work with (or have worked with in the past)? Do you spend time with the people you work with (or have worked with) outside of working hours?

8. Women exercise responsibility and authority differently than men do. Do you agree or disagree? Why? Please give several reasons for your position and illustrate these reasons with specific examples from your own experience or the experience of others.

J. **Reading Reconstruction: Read this paragraph as many times as you can in three minutes. Then, with your book closed, try to restate the ideas as clearly and completely as you can. (See Chapter 1 exercise for complete instructions.)**

Looking for Work Is a Job

In times of economic recession when jobs are hard to find, it is important to organize your job search carefully. Here are some tips to make your search more productive. First of all, consider that your job is getting a job. Work at getting a job every day for a regular number of hours. Next, ask people you know to suggest other people for you to talk to about a job. Also, at the end of every interview, ask the person who interviewed you for suggestions and names of people for you to contact. Offer to work part-time if a full-time job is not immediately available. Appear willing and eager. Most important, don't get discouraged and give up. Your job search will eventually be successful if you work hard at getting work.

Key words (to be written on the chalkboard):

economic	productive	suggestions	available
recession	consider	contact	willing
organize	regular	offer	eager
search	suggest	part-time	get discouraged
tips	interview	full-time	successful

K. Comprehension Check: On a separate piece of paper, write the numbers
1 through 10 on both sides. Mark one side "Test 1" and the other side
"Test 2." Read each statement and decide whether it is true or false.
Write "T" after true statements and "F" after false statements under
Test 1. After you have finished the comprehension check, turn Test 1
face down. Then read the article again and do the comprehension check
again under Test 2. Base your answers on the information in this article
only, even if you disagree with what the author said.

1. Men in the United States are now working in many kinds of jobs that
were once held entirely by women.

2. The number of male secretaries increased by almost 25% between 1972
and 1978.

3. The number of male nurses almost doubled between 1972 and 1978.

4. Men have entered female-dominated fields because jobs in these fields
are available.

5. Men have entered female-dominated fields because jobs in these fields
have more status.

6. Men have entered female-dominated fields because jobs in these fields
pay more.

7. Men sometimes face discrimination when they are working in female-
dominated fields.

8. Men in female-dominated fields tend to advance more quickly than
women do.

9. Women tend to be more assertive than men do at work.

10. Women are encouraged to take more responsibility than men do.

10

COPING WITH STRESS

[Dr. Hans Selye is a leading authority on stress. He has been doing research in this field for more than 40 years, and his book *Stress without Distress* is printed in nine languages. Dr. Selye is a member of the University of Montreal faculty, and he is now organizing the International Institute of Stress in Montreal.]

1. **Q:** *Dr. Selye, is it true that there is more stress in today's society than in years past?*
   A: People often ask me that question, sometimes comparing our lives with that of the cave man—who didn't have to worry about the stock market or the atomic bomb. They forget that the cave man worried about being eaten by a bear while he was asleep, or about dying of hunger—things that few people worry much about today. In the end, I doubt whether modern man experiences more distress than his ancestors. It's not that people suffer more stress today; it's just that they think they do.

2. **Q:** *But isn't everybody subject to stress?*
   A: That's right. Few studies have been done that permit me to answer in strictly objective, scientific terms, but as far as I can tell from talking to **diverse** groups—from businessmen to air-traffic controllers—everybody thinks he or she is under the greatest stress. The truth is that everybody actually is under stress because—and this may be shocking to **take**—if you really managed to avoid stress completely, you would be dead.

   different

   accept

3. **Q:** *Then stress is a normal state of affairs?*
   A: Yes, and it's important that people understand what they are talking about when they

speak about stress. Whenever anyone experiences something unpleasant, for lack of a better word they say they are under stress. Yet there is such a thing as pleasant stress—as in the case of the Olympic winner at the moment of his glory, or a conductor as his orchestra performs particularly well. They are just radiating excitement, and they are **secreting** all the stress hormones exactly the same as if they were **dejected** or had just heard of a death in the family. We call the pleasant or healthy kind "eustress" and the unpleasant or unhealthy kind "distress."

producing
upset

4. **Q:** *Are men and women equally subject to stress?*
    A: Certainly. Let me add that the more the "women's liberation" movement permits women to take what have usually been considered male jobs, the more women are subject to so-called male diseases, such as **cardiac infarctions**, gastric ulcers, and **hypertension**. They get the same satisfactions, too, of course, but at a price.

heart trouble
high blood
pressure

5. **Q:** *Before we go any further, exactly what is stress—plain worry, or something more than that?*
    A: In simple medical terms, I define stress as the response of the body to any demand. Stress is the state you are in, not the agent that produces it, which is called a stressor. Cold and heat, for example, are stressors. But in man, with his highly developed central nervous system, emotional stressors are the most frequent and the most important. The thing for the average person to remember is that all the demands that you make—whether on your brain or your liver or your muscles or your bones—cause stress. For example, stress can occur under deep anesthesia, when your emotions are not engaged, or in animals that have no nervous sytem, or even in plants.

simply

6. **Q:** *How can you tell when someone is under stress?*

A: There are two ways of **going about** this: One not **accessible** to the public is biochemical and neurological—measuring blood pressure, hormone levels, the electric activity of the brain, **and so on.** But there are other **indices** that anyone can judge. No two people react the same way, but the usual responses are an increase in pulse rate and an increased tendency to sweat. You will also become more irritable and will sometimes suffer insomnia, even long after the stressor agent is gone. You will usually become less capable of concentrating, and you will have an increased desire to move about. I was talking with a businessman this morning who asked if he could walk back and forth because he couldn't think well sitting down. That is a stress symptom everybody will know.

    doing
    open

    etc./measures

7. **Q:** *What are the more frequent causes of stress?*

A: One cannot generalize. They differ in various civilizations and historical time periods. At certain times, **pestilence** and hunger were the predominant causes. Another, then and now, is warfare or the fear of war. At the moment, I would say the most frequent causes of distress in man are psychological—that is to say, lack of adaptability, not having a code of behavior. One reason for this is that the satisfaction of religious codes has **diminished** in importance for mankind. So has the idea of being loyal to your monarch or leader. Even the satisfaction of **accumulating dollars** has been diminished by inflation.

    disease

    decreased

    saving money

8.   So one of the main problems for youngsters these days is that they have no motivation. It is not that they are stupid. Dropouts include the brightest. But they don't believe what they are

taught in school. And it's sometimes the most intelligent ones who then turn to drugs, alcohol, or other forms of abuse. They are very energetic, but they haven't anything to run for. The problem is expressed by the French writer Montaigne, who said: "No wind blows in favor of the ship that has no port of destination."

9.   **Q:**   *Stress is basically bad for you, isn't it?*
A: Not necessarily. It's the same as saying, "John is running a temperature." Well, who isn't? What you mean is that John is running too high a temperature. This brings us to two important words—"hyperstress" or too much stress and "hypostress" or not enough stress. Both words are relative. For me, it may not be enough; for you, it may be too much. But it is **inconceivable** that anyone should have no stress at all.

not possible

10.   Most people who are ambitious and want to accomplish something live on stress. They need it. I like to use examples from the animal world because there is a biological basis for what I say. If you take a turtle and force it to run as fast as a race horse, you will kill it. So it's useless to say to a turtle-type human that he must accomplish this because his father was famous and his grandfather before that. You can't make a race horse out of a turtle. But the **reverse** is also true. If you are the race-horse type, as most efficient business executives and politicians are, you have the **urge** to do many things and to express yourself. If you are told not to do anything, you are under terrible distress.

opposite

desire

too much
certainly

11.   **Q:**   *Does excessive stress do any harm?*
A: **By all means.** For instance, you can be bothered by your mother-in-law or your boss to the point where you suffer continuously, until you have gastric ulcers and hypertension and all the rest. When people say, "It gives me an ulcer" or "a pain in the neck" or "a migraine headache"

to do certain things, it's not just a way of talking. It actually does happen. **Chronic** exposure to stress over a long time may cause serious diseases —cardiovascular disease, heart attacks, mental breakdowns—the typical stress diseases, we call them.

repeated

12. **Q:** *How can people cope with stress?*
A: The secret is not to avoid stress but to "do your own thing." That is an expression to which I fully subscribe. It implies doing what you like to do and what you were made to do at your own rate. Medicine can help. There are good drugs for high blood pressure, for instance. But for most people, it is really a matter of learning how to live, how to behave in various situations, to decide: "Do I really want to take over my father's business or be a musician?" If you really want to be a musician, then be one.

handle

TURN TO COMPREHENSION CHECK AT END OF CHAPTER

READING TIMES:	READING SPEED:
1st reading _____ minutes	9 minutes = 139 wpm
2nd reading _____ minutes	8 minutes = 157 wpm
	7 minutes = 179 wpm
	6 minutes = 209 wpm
	5 minutes = 251 wpm

A. Analysis of Ideas and Relationships: Circle the letter next to the best answer.

1. The main idea of paragraph 1 is that:
   a. people in all ages have suffered stress.
   b. cave men didn't have to worry about the stock market or the atomic bomb.
   c. today's people suffer more stress than cave men did.

2. According to paragraph 2:
   a. people should try to avoid stress completely.
   b. everybody experiences stress.
   c. air-traffic controllers experience more stress than businessmen do.

3. Put the following statements into logical order. Then refer to paragraph 7 to check your work.
   a. "One reason for this is that the satisfaction of religious codes has diminished in importance for mankind."
   b. "At the moment, I would say the most frequent causes of distress in man are psychological—that is to say, lack of adaptability, not having a code of behavior."
   c. "So has the idea of being loyal to your monarch or leader."

4. Which statement is NOT necessarily true?
   a. Stress is normal.
   b. Stress is bad for you.
   c. Stress can shorten your life.

5. The subject of paragraph 7 is:
   a. causes of distress in modern times.
   b. the importance of religion.
   c. the importance of loyalty to a leader.

6. The main idea of paragraph 11 is that:
   a. when people say, "It gives me an ulcer," they don't mean it.
   b. you should try not to be bothered by people.
   c. too much stress can be harmful.

7. The main idea of this article is that:
   a. you should try to avoid stress whenever possible.
   b. you should not try to avoid stress, but you should learn how to live in the best way for you.
   c. you should never follow in your father's footsteps.

8. If you told Dr. Selye that your father wanted you to become a doctor, what do you think Dr. Selye would ask you?
   a. "What kind of doctor does he want you to be?"
   b. "What do *you* want to be?"
   c. "Do you respect your father?"

   Please explain your answer.

9. Dr. Selye's views on stress are important because:
   a. he is a doctor.
   b. he has been doing research in his specialty—stress—for more than 40 years.
   c. both a. and b.

10. This article is an example of:
    a. technical writing. It would probably appear in a journal written for scientists.
    b. an interview. It would probably appear in a newspaper or magazine written for the general public.
    c. an editorial. It would probably appear on the editorial page of a newspaper or magazine.

    Please explain your answer.

B. Interpretation of Words and Phrases: Circle the letter next to the best answer.

1. "It's not that people suffer more stress today; it's just that they think they **do.**"
   a. do more things
   b. do not suffer more stress
   c. suffer more stress

2. "The more the 'women's liberation' movement permits women to take what have usually been considered male jobs, the more women are subject to so-called male diseases, such as cardiac infarctions, gastric ulcers, and hypertension." This statement suggests that:
   a. these diseases may be connected to the high stress of the job rather than to the sex of the person doing the job.
   b. men are more subject to stress than women are for certain biological reasons relating to their sex.
   c. women are naturally less affected by stress than men are regardless of the type of work they are doing.

3. "Stress is the **state** you are in."
   a. geographical area
   b. condition
   c. position

4. "No wind blows in favor of the ship that has no port of destination."
   a. You must have wind in order to sail.
   b. It is impossible for a ship not to have a port of destination.
   c. Nothing can help you reach a goal if you don't have a goal.

5. "Most people who are ambitious and want to accomplish something live on stress. They need **it**."
   a. accomplishment
   b. ambition
   c. stress

6. "If you take a turtle and force it to run as fast as a race horse, you will kill it." In the context of this article, this means that:
   a. race horses are better than turtles.
   b. turtles are slower than race horses.
   c. you should not force a person to do something that he or she is not made to do.

7. "Does excessive stress do any harm? **By all means**."
   a. Certainly.
   b. In any way possible.
   c. Understandably.

8. "It **actually** does happen."
   a. at the present time
   b. really
   c. sometimes

9. "Chronic exposure to stress over a long time may cause serious diseases." This means that:
   a. chronic exposure to stress definitely causes serious diseases.
   b. it is possible that chronic exposure to stress will cause serious diseases.
   c. there is no relationship between chronic exposure to stress and disease.

10. Is stress bad for you? **Not necessarily**.
    a. Maybe yes and maybe no.
    b. Stress is not necessary.
    c. Stress is necessary.

C. **Synonyms: From this list, choose a synonym for the word in bold type in each sentence.**

agree with	to perspire	can do
affected by	to adjust to	too much
to keep away from	to handle	repeated
produces		

1. **Excessive** stress is bad for you.

2. Are men and women equally **subject to** stress?

3. It is important to learn how **to cope with** stress.

4. There is no way **to avoid** stress completely.

5. I **subscribe to** the philosophy of "doing your own thing."

6. I think that **I am capable of doing** the job well.

7. **Chronic** exposure to stress over a long time may cause serious diseases.

8. Your body **secretes** hormones when you are under stress.

9. When you are under stress, you are likely **to sweat.**

10. In order to survive, you have to be able **to adapt to** changing conditions.

D. **Prepositions and Verb-Completers: Write any appropriate preposition or verb-completer in the blank spaces.**

1. Cave men suffered _____ stress too.

2. They worried _____ being eaten _____ a bear or dying _____ hunger.

3. The causes _____ stress differ _____ various civilizations and historical periods.

4. One _____ the main problems _____ our youngsters is that they have no motivation.

5. No wind blows _____ favor _____ the ship that has no port _____ destination.

6. Most people who are ambitious and want _____ accomplish something live _____ stress.

7. Repeated exposure _____ stress _____ a long period _____ time may cause serious diseases.

8. People can learn how _____ cope _____ stress.

9. They should learn how _____ behave _____ various situations.

10. The most important thing is _____ have a code _____ behavior _____ life.

E. Cloze Exercise: Fill in the blanks with any appropriate word.

People often ask me _____ question, sometimes comparing
(1)
our _____ with that of the cave _____ —who didn't have
(2)   (3)
to _____ about the stock market _____ the atomic bomb.
(4)   (5)
They _____ that the cave man _____ about being eaten by
(6)   (7)
_____ bear while he was _____, or about dying of
(8)   (9)
_____ —things that few people _____ much about today.
(10)   (11)
In _____ end, I doubt whether _____ man experiences
(12)   (13)
more distress _____ his ancestors. It's not _____ people
(14)   (15)
suffer more stress _____; it's just that they _____ they do.
(16)   (17)

F. Punctuation Exercise: Write in capital letters, periods, and commas where needed.

but isn't everybody subject to stress that's right few studies have been done that permit me to answer in strictly objective scientific terms but as far as i can tell from talking to diverse groups—from businessmen to air-traffic controllers—everybody thinks he or she is under the greatest stress the truth is that everybody actually is under stress because—and this may be shocking to take—if you really managed to avoid stress completely you would be dead

G. **Word Forms: Choose the correct word form to fit into each sentence. Use appropriate verb tenses, singular or plural forms for nouns, and passive voice where necessary.**

1. **pleasure, to please, pleasant, pleasantly**
   a. I accepted his invitation with _____ .
   b. The weather in the Caribbean is very _____ .
   c. I am sure your letter will _____ her.
   d. She looked up and smiled _____ as he came in.

2. **stress, distress, to stress, stressful**
   a. Dr. Selye _____ the importance of knowing how to live.
   b. The agent that produces _____ is called a stressor.
   c. Unhealthy or unpleasant stress is called _____ .
   d. _____ situations are not necessarily bad.

3. **understanding, to understand, understanding, understandable, understandingly, understandably**
   a. Of course I _____ how you feel.
   b. Your anger is _____ .
   c. You were _____ angry.
   d. It is important to treat people with respect and _____ .
   e. She gave him an _____ look.
   f. She looked at him _____ .

4. **nerve, nervousness, nervous, nervously**
   a. She had never given a speech before, and she was very _____ .
   b. She looked out at the large crowd _____ .
   c. She tried to hide her _____ .
   d. She took several deep breaths to quiet her _____ .

5. **response, to respond, responsive, responsively**
   a. His answer was long, but it was not _____ .
   b. When Mr. Lebron finally _____ , everyone listened carefully.
   c. I wrote to Allan immediately, but I did not get a _____ .
   d. She didn't say anything, but she smiled _____ .

6. **basis, to base, basic, basically**
   a. _____ , stress is a normal part of life.
   b. You must take the _____ courses in mathematics before you take the advanced ones.
   c. What facts do you _____ your argument upon?
   d. What is the _____ of your argument?

7. **definition, to define, definite, definitely**
   a. Too much stress can _____ cause physical problems.
   b. How do you _____ "stress"?
   c. What is the _____ of "stress"?
   d. It is _____ that too much stress is harmful.

8. **relative, relation, relationship, to relate, relative, relatively**
   a. Most of her _____ still live in Czechoslovakia.
   b. Tell me, what is the _____ between them?
   c. There have been _____ few plane crashes this year.
   d. The terms "distress" and "eustress" are _____ .
   e. He did not do very well on the spatial _____ exam.
   f. Would you please _____ that amazing story again?

9. **seriousness, serious, seriously**
   a. Anne is _____ interested in economics.
   b. She has always been a _____ student.
   c. Her teachers and classmates are impressed by her _____ .

0. **energy, energetic, energetically**
   a. Children have so much _____ .
   b. The most _____ person I have ever met was only five years old.
   c. She was always running around _____ .

H. Sentence Scramble: Make a sentence out of each group of words.

1. state – stress – a – normal – is

2. pleasant – is – a – thing – such – there – stress – as

3. is – necessarily – stress – not – bad – you – for

4. who – ambitious – are – people – stress – on – live

5. for – how – to – learn – live – to – important – is – it – people

I. **Topics for Discussion and Composition:**

1. According to Dr. Selye, the causes of stress are not necessarily the same in all cultures. In some cultures, there are severe economic pressures; in others, there may be the threat of war. What are the main causes of stress in your culture? Why? Please give specific examples of these causes of stress from either your own experience or the experience of others. How do people in your country try to cope with stress?

2. It has been said that people in the modern world feel that stress is unhealthy, and they try to avoid it. Do you think this is true? Why? Or why not? Please give several specific examples to support your opinion.

3. Stress can be pleasant ("eustress"); please describe a situation in which you experienced a pleasant kind of stress. Why was the situation stressful? What finally happened?

4. Have you ever felt that you needed more stress in your life? Would you change your life to make it more stressful? How? Why?

5. In the year 2000, the main cause(s) of stress will be _____ . Please complete this sentence, explain, and give specific examples. How will people try to cope with this stress?

6. Children should be protected as much as possible from stress. Do you agree or disagree? Why? Please give reasons for your position and specific examples to illustrate your reasons.

J.   Reading Reconstruction: Read this paragraph as many times as you can in three minutes. Then, with your book closed, try to restate the ideas as clearly and completely as you can. (See Chapter 1 exercise for complete instructions.)

That Happy Feeling

In our modern world, we think that happiness is our natural state and that we should avoid stress whenever possible. We think that stress is not good because it may be unpleasant. We might feel pain, and we think that pain is bad. After all, it hurts. But can we have happiness without pain? Can we have joy without sorrow? By trying to feel good all the time, are we, in fact, losing the ability to feel?

Key words (to be written on the chalkboard):

happiness	state	stress	pain	ability
natural	avoid	unpleasant	losing	feel

K. Comprehension Check: On a separate piece of paper, write the numbers 1 through 10 on both sides. Mark one side "Test 1" and the other side "Test 2." Read each statement and decide whether it is true or false. Write "T" after true statements and "F" after false statements under Test 1. After you have finished the comprehension check, turn Test 1 face down. Then read the article again and do the comprehension check again under Test 2. Base your answers on the information in this article *only*, even if you disagree with what the author said.

1. Modern man faces more stress than the cave man did.

2. Stress is a normal state.

3. Stress is always unpleasant.

4. Women and men are equally affected by stress.

5. The causes of stress are the same in all civilizations and periods.

6. The most common causes of stress today are economic.

7. Young people face less stress than older people do.

8. Too much stress can cause disease.

9. Different people have different stress needs.

10. People should try to avoid stress.

11

THE SPACE PROGRAM:
IS IT WORTH IT?

[This panel discussion took place in a college class in New York City in April 1981 shortly after the successful mission of the U.S. space shuttle, the Columbia. This mission marked the first time a spaceship had been sent out into space and then landed back on earth so that it could be used again later for more flights. Many people considered this to be a tremendous advance for the space program. But some people felt that the cost was too high. This discussion reveals some of the differences of opinion on the importance and the cost of the space program. The discussion is moderated by the classroom professor, and the students are simply referred to as *A* and *B*.]

1   *Moderator:* Let me begin by saying that everyone is very excited about the successful mission of the space shuttle, the Columbia. It is the first time that a spacecraft has been successfully landed back on earth after a space **voyage**, and this means that this spaceship can be used again on other missions. Obviously, there will be a tremendous saving because we won't have to send up a completely new spacecraft on every mission. Also, we will be able to bring cargo safely back from space in the future—and this offers exciting possibilities from the scientists' point of view.

trip

2   However, there are differences of opinion about the space program. Many people feel that it costs too much. Today we are going to hear two different points of view on the space program. First, let's hear from someone who is strongly in favor of the space program and who doesn't believe that it costs too much. And then we'll hear the other side. Would you please begin, *A*?

3   *A:* Yes. I believe that the space program is one of the most important programs the United States has and that we ought to spend even more money on it than is being spent right now. The space program is an investment in the future, and it has great potential to make life on earth better.

4   *Moderator:* Thank you, *A.* And now, *B,* would you please tell us your position briefly. Then we'll discuss the points of difference between you.

5   *B:* First of all, I want to make it clear that I am not against the space program. I just think it costs too much and that society would benefit more from improved social programs than from space exploration. If we could have both—an elaborate space program and really good social welfare programs—I would be very happy. But if we have to choose, I am in favor of choosing to invest in social welfare programs. People need food, shelter, jobs, education—**bread-and-butter** necessities. Space programs won't provide these basic essentials of a decent life.

basic

6   *Moderator:* So you are saying, *B,* that if we have to choose between investing in social welfare programs and the space program, we should choose social programs because they meet people's immediate needs. Is that right?

7   *B:* Yes, that's right. I'm not against the space program in theory. I just think it is too expensive and that we can't afford it. It's a luxury. The space shuttle cost more than 20 billion dollars. That's a lot of money. And who benefits?

8   *Moderator:* Would you like to answer that, *A*? After all, who benefits from the space shuttle? Does the space program really help us here on earth, or is it simply an exciting adventure program, something that looks good on TV?

9   *A:* I think we all benefit from the space shuttle in very important ways. The space shuttle proves that we can go into space and then land safely back on earth again. Now we will be able to transport cargo back and

forth. We can build laboratories in space and do experiments there that we can't do here on earth because of the earth's gravity. We can produce chemicals and medicines there that we cannot produce here on earth, and these substances will be tremendously valuable to us. We can also set up a really effective system of defense in space to protect our country from foreign attack. Yes, all of us in the United States are going to benefit a great deal from the space program.

10   *B:* But you're talking about **maybes** in the future.   possibilities
I'm talking about *now.* We need better medical and health services *now,* better programs for the elderly *now,* better day-care centers for children *now,* better youth services *now. We need better programs for people now*—not just some vague possibility of scientific advances in the future. You're talking about **pie in the**   a dream
sky.

11   *A:* I don't agree. I think a country always has to look to the future in order to be great and to stay great. I think our social services are good enough now. I think we can make life better for more people by investing in the space program. I think the results will greatly improve everyday life here on earth. For example, it's possible that we could collect solar energy for use here on earth. We might be able to solve one of our biggest problems, the energy problem, this way. We wouldn't have to rely on an uncertain supply of oil and coal then. And this would be a huge advance for everyone on earth.

12   *B:* You're still talking about *possibilities* in the future. Meanwhile, we have people who don't have enough to eat, who don't have a place to live, who can't afford to get a good education. I think the U.S. government could set a wonderful example for the whole world by giving **priority** to social programs. Other   preference
governments would look at the United States and see that we are investing in our people. And nothing is more important than the people in a country.

13   *A:* Let me just say again that I think that investing in the space program is also an investment in the

greatly

people. I think that the long-range benefits of the space program can **drastically** change life on this earth for everyone. I think that mankind has the chance to move ahead, to make real progress toward a better life, and that this will happen as a result of scientific achievements in space. I think if we invest more in our existing social programs, we will be thinking only about today and forgetting tomorrow. We won't be moving forward.

14   *B:* And I think that if we invest too heavily in our space program, we will be forgetting today. After all, people can't eat dreams. People have to live on something more nourishing than hope.

15   *A:* But we shouldn't forget that people need hope too.

16   *Moderator:* I want to thank both of you for the interesting points you have made. It seems to me that your disagreement is not over the space program and its quality and potential for the future. Your disagreement is simply over how much we should invest in it and whether we should give priority to the space program rather than to social welfare programs. Thank you both again for sharing your views with us. I'm sure you've given us all a great deal of food for thought.

TURN TO COMPREHENSION CHECK AT END OF CHAPTER

READING TIMES:
1st reading _____ minutes
2nd reading _____ minutes

READING SPEED:
8 minutes = 120 wpm
7 minutes = 137 wpm
6 minutes = 160 wpm
5 minutes = 190 wpm

A. **Analysis of Ideas and Relationships: Circle the letter next to the best answer.**

1. "The Space Program: Is It Worth It?" is in the form of:
   a. an editorial.
   b. a lecture.
   c. a panel discussion.

2. The participants in the discussion, *A* and *B*:
   a. disagree over how much the U.S. government should invest in the space program.
   b. agree on how much the U.S. government should invest in the space program.
   c. agree that the U.S. government should give priority to social welfare programs.

3. Speaker *A* is in favor of:
   a. giving social welfare programs priority over the space program.
   b. giving equal attention to social welfare programs and the space program.
   c. giving the space program priority over the social welfare programs.

4. Speaker *B* is in favor of:
   a. giving social welfare programs priority over the space program.
   b. giving equal attention to social welfare programs and the space program.
   c. giving the space program priority over the social welfare programs.

5. The moderator:
   a. obviously agrees with Speaker *A*.
   b. obviously agrees with Speaker *B*.
   c. tries to be fair and impartial to both *A* and *B*.

6. Why was the mission of the Columbia important?
   a. It was the first time a spacecraft had gone from the earth into space.
   b. It was the first time a spacecraft had landed back on earth again, and this meant that the same spacecraft could be used again for other space missions.
   c. It was the first time a spacecraft had landed safely on the moon.

7. Which statement is NOT true?
   a. Speaker *B* is not against the space program in theory.
   b. Speaker *A* believes that the existing social welfare programs are good enough.
   c. Speaker *A* believes that the space program costs too much.

8. Speaker *B* believes that Speaker *A*:
   a. is putting too much emphasis on the future and not enough on the present.
   b. is putting too much emphasis on the present and not enough on the future.
   c. is not clear about whether to emphasize the present or the future.

9. Speaker *A* believes that Speaker *B*:
   a. is putting too much emphasis on the future and not enough on the present.
   b. is putting too much emphasis on the present and not enough on the future.
   c. is not clear about whether to emphasize the present or the future.

10. This article shows:
   a. why the U.S. government should give priority to the space program.
   b. why the U.S. government should give priority to the social welfare programs.
   c. differences of opinion on the importance and the cost of the space program.

B. **Interpretation of Words and Phrases: Circle the letter next to the best answer.**

1. "First, let's hear from someone who is strongly in favor of the space program... **and then we'll hear the other side.**"
   a. and then we'll hear from someone sitting on the side
   b. and then we'll hear from someone who has a different opinion of the space program
   c. and then we'll hear from someone who is also in favor of the space program

2. "The space program has great **potential** to make life on earth better."
   a. possibilities
   b. power
   c. appeal

3. "Would you please tell us your position **briefly.**"
   a. in a few words
   b. in detail
   c. with proof

4. "I am not **against** the space program."
   a. in favor of
   b. opposed to
   c. in agreement with

5. "People need **bread-and-butter** necessities."
   a. basic
   b. food
   c. many

6. "We should choose social programs because they **meet** people's immediate needs."
   a. become acquainted with
   b. satisfy
   c. go together with

7. "But you're talking about **maybes** in the future."
   a. certainties
   b. possibilities
   c. probabilities

8. "We need better programs for people now—not just some **vague** possibility of scientific advances in the future."
   a. definite
   b. clear
   c. unclear

9. "You're talking about pie in the sky."
   a. You're talking about a sweet dessert in heaven.
   b. You're talking about a fantasy.
   c. You're talking about food in space.

10. "A country always **has to look to** the future."
    a. has to watch
    b. has to think about
    c. has to see

C. Synonyms: From this list, choose a synonym for the word in bold type in each sentence.

very large	greatly	accomplishment
possibilities	do (you) support	space flights
basic necessities	preference	equipment and materials
housing		

1. **Are you in favor of** spending more money on the space program?

2. The Columbia can be used again on other **missions.**

3. Reusable spacecrafts have great **potential.**

4. It will be possible to bring **cargo** back from space.

5. People have certain basic needs: food, clothing, and **shelter.**

6. It is important to have the **essentials** of a decent life.

7. Life on earth could be **drastically** changed by accomplishments in space.

8. The successful landing of the Columbia back on earth was a great **achievement.**

9. Do you think we should give **priority** to the space program or to social welfare programs?

10. The budget for the Columbia flight was **huge.**

D. Prepositions and Verb-Completers: Write any appropriate preposition or verb-completer in the blank spaces.

1. Everyone was very excited _____ the successful mission _____ the spaceship, the Columbia.

2. This was the first time that a spacecraft had been successfully landed _____ _____ earth _____ a space voyage.

3. However, there were differences _____ opinion _____ the space program.

4. This panel discussion represented two different points _____ view _____ the space program.

5. Speaker *A* felt that the space program was one _____ the most important programs the United States has.

6. Speaker *B* said that he was not _____ the space program _____ theory.

7. He just felt that society would benefit more _____ improved social programs.

8. He said that he was _____ favor _____ giving priority _____ social programs.

9. Speaker *A* believed that it would be better _____ invest _____ the space program.

10. He said that he believed that the space program is also an investment _____ the people.

E. Cloze Exercise: Fill in the blanks with any appropriate word.

Let me begin by _____ that everyone is very _____
         (1)   (2)
about the successful mission _____ the space shuttle, the
                   (3)
Columbia. _____ is the first time _____ a spacecraft has
       (4)   (5)
been _____ landed back on earth _____ a space voyage,
     (6)   (7)
and _____ means that this spaceship _____ be used again
   (8)   (9)
on _____ missions. Obviously, there will _____ a tre-
    (10)   (11)
mendous saving because _____ won't have to send _____
           (12)   (13)
a completely new spacecraft _____ every mission. Also, we
          (14)
_____ be able to bring _____ safely back from space
  (15)   (16)
_____ the future—and this _____ exciting possibilities
  (17)   (18)
from the _____ ' point of view.
      (19)

F. **Punctuation Exercise: Write in capital letters, period, and commas where needed.**

let me just say again that i think that investing in the space program is also an investment in the people i think that the long-range benefits of the space program can drastically change life on this earth for everyone i think that mankind has the chance to move ahead to make real progress toward a better life and that this will happen as a result of scientific achievements in space i think if we invest more in our existing social programs we will be thinking only about today and forgetting tomorrow we won't be moving forward

G. **Word Forms: Choose the correct word form to fit into each sentence. Use appropriate verb tenses, singular or plural forms for nouns, and passive voice where necessary.**

1. **space, to space**
   a. Do you think we should give priority to the _____ program?
   b. Please double _____ that report. In other words, type on every other line.

2. **beginner, beginning, to begin**
   a. I loved the _____ of that movie.
   b. He finally _____ to understand after he had thought about the problem for a few days.
   c. This book is not for a _____ .

3. **success, to succeed, successful, successfully**
   a. It was a _____ project.
   b. No one was surprised by her _____ .
   c. How did you _____ ?
   d. The Columbia landed back on earth _____ .

4. **investor, investment, to invest**
   a. Did you ever _____ in the stock market?
   b. Think carefully before you make a large _____ .
   c. She is the principal _____ in the company.

5. **theory, theoretical, theoretically**
   a. In _____ , I agree with your proposal, but I am not sure if it will actually work.
   b. Have you studied the _____ aspects?
   c. _____ , the plan was a good one.

6. **society, to socialize, social, socially**
   a. Is the space program important to _____ ?
   b. It is not _____ acceptable to chew gum in certain situations.
   c. I knew him at work, but we never _____ after work.
   d. It was an important _____ event.

7. **expense, to spend, expensive, expensively**
   a. His apartment is comfortable, but it is not _____ furnished.
   b. Don't _____ all your money immediately.
   c. It was an _____ car.
   d. I didn't consider the _____ of the trip carefully, so I ran out of money before I arrived home.

8. **luxury, luxurious, luxuriously**
   a. He lived in an atmosphere of great _____ .
   b. His mansion was _____ furnished.
   c. He lived in a _____ manner.

9. **immediate, immediately**
   a. I have no _____ plans.
   b. Please write back _____ .

10. **benefit, to benefit, beneficial, beneficially**
    a. Who will _____ from that program?
    b. Will people be _____ affected?
    c. What are the _____ of the program?
    d. Is the program _____ ?

H. Sentence Scramble: Make a sentence out of each group of words.

1. should – government – give – to – space – the – program – the – priority

2. invest – social – programs – some – people – government – more – the – think – should – in

3. these – benefit – people – think – programs – that – social – people – more

4. luxury – space – they – program – that – think – the – is – a

5. others – program – important – future – the – for – development – think – that – space – is

I. Topics for Discussion and Composition:

1. Speaker *A* says: "I believe that the space program is one of the most important programs the United States has and that we ought to spend even more money on it than is being spent right now." Do you agree or disagree? Why? Please support your reasons with specific examples.

2. Speaker *B* says: "I am in favor of choosing to invest in social welfare programs. People need food, shelter, jobs, education—bread-and-butter necessities. Space programs won't provide these basic essentials of a decent life." Do you agree or disagree? Why? Please support your reasons with specific examples.

3. What makes a country or a society "great"? Please explain what you mean by *great* and then discuss just two or three features of a great society. Please give specific examples if possible. What society or societies in the present-day world do you consider great? Why?

4. Do you think that human (or human-like) life exists in other places in the universe? Why? Or why not? Please give several reasons for your answer.

5. Suppose that you are writing to a person in outer space and you are describing the three greatest achievements of earthlings (people who live on earth). What are mankind's three greatest achievements in your opinion? Why? How has life been affected by these achievements? (Note: please limit yourself to describing three achievements.)

J. **Reading Reconstruction: Read this paragraph as many times as you can in three minutes. Then, with your book closed, try to restate the ideas as clearly and completely as you can. (See Chapter 1 exercise for complete instructions.)**

Is Anybody Out There?

On clear nights, people have always looked up at the stars and planets and wondered, "What is it like up there? Is anybody out there? Are we the only ones?" We still don't know the answers to all these questions, although each space voyage takes us a little closer to finding out. Now we know that the moon is NOT made of green cheese, and we know that there aren't any little people on Mars. But someplace way out there, there may be others. And maybe, just maybe, on clear nights, they look out at the earth and wonder, "What's it like down there? Is anybody out there? Are we the only ones?"

Key words (to be written on the chalkboard):

stars	space	green cheese
planets	voyage	Mars
wondered	moon	earth

K. **Comprehension Check:** On a separate piece of paper, write the numbers 1 through 10 on both sides. Mark one side "Test 1" and the other side "Test 2." Read each statement and decide whether it is true or false. Write "T" after true statements and "F" after false statements under Test 1. After you have finished the comprehension check, turn Test 1 face down. Then read the article again and do the comprehension check again under Test 2. Base your answers on the information in this article *only*, even if you disagree with what the author said.

1. The Columbia was the first spacecraft to land on the moon.

2. The Columbia was the first spacecraft to orbit (circle) the earth.

3. The Columbia was the first spacecraft to land safely back on earth after a space flight so that it could be reused for later space flights.

4. Speaker *A* is strongly in favor of the space program.

5. Speaker *B* is not opposed to the space program, but he feels that it costs too much.

6. The space shuttle (the Columbia mission) cost about 20 million dollars.

7. Experiments can be done in space that cannot be done on earth because of gravity.

8. Speaker *B* thinks that the government should give priority to social programs.

9. Speaker *A* thinks that the existing social programs are satisfactory as they are.

10. In the end, both speakers agree that the space program should be given priority over social programs.

12

LIFE WITHOUT FUEL

[Isaac Asimov is a noted scientist and science fiction writer. He has a remarkable gift for being able to explain complex science phenomena in ways that the ordinary person can easily understand. Asimov was recently asked to imagine and describe what would happen to everyday life in 1997 if fuel really began running out. Asimov explains that this "is a picture of the worst, of waste continuing, of oil running out, of nothing in its place, of world population continuing to rise."]

1   It's 1997, and it's raining, and you'll have to walk to work again. Any given subway train breaks down one morning out of five. The buses are gone, and on a day like today, bicycles slosh and slide.

2   Lucky you have a job in **demolition**. It's slow and dirty work, but steady. The fading structures of a decaying city are the great mineral mines and hardware shops of the nation. Break them down and reuse the parts. Coal is too difficult to dig up and transport to give us energy in the amounts we need, nuclear fission is judged to be too dangerous, the hoped-for breakthrough toward nuclear fusion never took place, and **solar** batteries are too expensive to maintain in sufficient quantity.

tearing buildings down

sun

3   Anyone older than ten can remember automobiles. At first, the price of gasoline climbed—way up. Finally, only the **well-to-do** drove, and that was too clear an indication that they were **filthy rich**; so any automobile on a city street was overturned and burned. The cars **vanished**, becoming part of the metal resource.

rich people
extremely rich

disappeared

4   There are advantages in 1997, if you want to look for them. The air is cleaner, and there seem to be fewer

colds. The crime rate has dropped. With the police car too expensive, policemen are back on their **beats.** More important, the streets are full. Legs are king, and people walk everywhere far into the night. There is mutual protection in crowds.

foot patrols

5   If the weather isn't too cold, people sit out front. If it is hot, the open air is the only air conditioning they get. At least the street lights still burn. Indoors, few people can afford to keep lights burning after supper.

6   As for the winter—well, it is inconvenient to be cold, with most of what furnace fuel is allowed **hoarded** for the dawn. But sweaters are popular indoor **wear.** Showers are not an everyday luxury. Lukewarm sponge baths must do, and if the air is not always very **fragrant** in the human vicinity, the automobile fumes are gone.

saved

clothing

pleasant smelling

7   It is worse in the suburbs, which were born with the auto, lived with the auto, and are dying with the auto. Suburbanites form associations that assign turns to the **procurement** and distribution of food. Pushcarts **creak** from house to house along the **posh** suburban roads, and every bad snowstorm is a disaster. It isn't easy to **hoard** enough food to last till the roads are open. There is not much refrigeration except for the snow-banks, and then the dogs must be fought off.

buying

squeak/ elegant

store

8   What energy is left must be conserved for agri-culture. The great car factories make trucks and farm machinery almost exclusively. The American popula-tion isn't going up much anymore, but the food supply must be kept high even though the prices and difficulty of distribution force each American to eat less. Food is needed for export to pay for some **trickles** of oil and for other resources.

tiny stream

9   The rest of the world is not as lucky as we are. They're starving out there because earth's population has continued to rise. The population on earth is 5.5 billion—up by 1.5 billion since 1977—and, outside the United States and Europe, not more than one in five has enough to eat at any given time. There is a high infant **mortality** rate.

death

10   It's more than just starvation, though. There are those who manage to survive on barely enough to keep the body working, and that proves to be not enough for the brain. It is estimated that nearly two billion people in the world are permanently brain-damaged by under-nutrition, and the number is growing.

11   At least the big armies are gone. Only the United States and the Soviet Union can maintain a few tanks, planes, and ships—which they dare not move for fear of biting into limited fuel reserves.

12   Machines must be replaced by human muscle and **beasts of burden.** People are working longer hours, and—with lighting restricted, television only three hours a night, new books few and printed in small editions—what is there to do with **leisure**? Work, sleep, and eating are the great **trinity** of 1997, and only the first two are **guaranteed.**

animals that carry things

numbers/free time/three things/certain

13   Where will it end? It must end in a return to the days before 1800, to the days before the fossil fuels powered a **vast** machine industry and technology. It must end in subsistence farming and in a world popu-lation reduced by starvation, disease, and violence to less than a billion.

huge

14   And what can we do to **prevent** all this now?

stop

15   Now? In 1997? Almost nothing.

TURN TO COMPREHENSION CHECK AT END OF CHAPTER

READING TIMES:
1st reading _____ minutes
2nd reading_____ minutes

READING SPEED:
8 minutes = 120 wpm
7 minutes = 136 wpm
6 minutes = 160 wpm
5 minutes = 190 wpm
4 minutes = 240 wpm

A. Analysis of Ideas and Relationships: Circle the letter next to the best answer.

1. "Life without Fuel" is:
   a. a scientific study of life in 1997.
   b. an imaginary account of life in 1997.
   c. a history of life in 1997.

2. According to paragraph 2, a good kind of job to have is in:
   a. demolition.
   b. a gasoline station.
   c. construction.

   Why? Please explain your answer.

3. Which statement is NOT true according to this article?
   a. Energy will be expensive and in short supply.
   b. There will be more cars than ever in 1997.
   c. The air will be cleaner in 1997.

4. Paragraph 4 discusses:
   a. the advantages of life in 1997.
   b. the disadvantages of life in 1997.
   c. the advantages of life today.

5. Paragraph 5 shows that, in 1997, people will:
   a. use less electricity than they do today.
   b. use more electricity than they do today.
   c. not use any electricity.

6. According to paragraph 7, in 1997, life in the suburbs will be:
   a. much easier than life in the cities.
   b. more difficult than life in the cities.
   c. about the same as life in the cities.

   Why? Please explain your answer.

7. Why will America need to export food in 1997?
   a. Because they will have too much food for their own use.
   b. Because the farmers will want to make a lot of money.
   c. Because they will need money to buy oil.

8. How would you compare the rest of the world with America in 1997?
   a. America will be luckier than the rest of the world.
   b. The rest of the world will be luckier than America.
   c. Everyone will be well off.

9. The tone of this article is:
   a. pessimistic.
   b. optimistic.
   c. cheerful.

   Please explain your answer.

10. The problems Isaac Asimov describes in this article are caused by:
    a. a lack of fuel.
    b. the wrong kind of fuel.
    c. too much fuel.

    Please explain your answer.

B. Interpretation of Words and Phrases: Circle the letter next to the best answer.

1. "Any given subway train breaks down one morning out of five."
   a. In general, subway trains break down one morning out of every five mornings.
   b. A subway train that is given to you breaks down one morning out of five mornings.
   c. A subway train that you give breaks down one morning out of every five mornings.

2. "Lucky you have a job in demolition."
   a. You have a lucky job.
   b. As luck would have it, you have a job in demolition.
   c. You are lucky that you have a job in demolition.

3. "The hoped-for breakthrough toward nuclear fusion never took place."
   a. The nuclear explosion never happened.
   b. The scientific advance in the field of nuclear fusion that people hoped for never happened.
   c. The break in nuclear fusion hopefully never happened.

4. "At first, the price of gasoline climbed—way up."
   a. At first, the price of gasoline increased greatly.
   b. At first, the price of gasoline climbed high into the sky.
   c. The first price of gasoline was high.

5. "Legs are king, and people walk everywhere."
   a. There is a king now, and he makes people walk everywhere.
   b. Walking is the most important form of transportation, and people walk everywhere.
   c. It is considered a good thing that people walk everywhere.

6. "As for the winter—well, it is inconvenient to be cold."
   a. In the winter, it is convenient to be cold.
   b. It is more inconvenient to be cold in winter than in summer.
   c. Referring to winter, it is not convenient to be cold.

7. "Sweaters are popular indoor wear."
   a. Many people wear sweaters in the house.
   b. Sweaters are more popular indoors than outdoors.
   c. Sweaters are worn by popular people.

8. "Lukewarm sponge baths must do."
   a. People take baths with warm sponges.
   b. People have to manage by washing themselves with a little bit of warm water.
   c. People don't like to take hot baths, so they take warm ones.

9. "At least the big armies are gone."
   a. Finally, the big armies are gone.
   b. The least of the big armies are gone.
   c. One good thing is that the big armies are gone.

10. "Where will it end?"
    a. What will be the final result?
    b. What is the destination?
    c. How far is it to the end?

C. **Synonyms: From this list, choose a synonym for the word in bold type in each sentence.**

pass it around	energy from sunrays
control	don't have enough money
only	survive
tiny stream	say with certainty
torn down	extremely

1. I **can't afford** to buy a new car.

2. There will be two food committees; one will buy the food, and the other will **distribute** it to the people.

3. Cars were owned **exclusively** by very rich people.

4. I can **guarantee** that there will be problems if oil runs out.

5. It is very dry, and there is only a **trickle** of water in that brook.

6. How long can we **last** without food and water?

7. That building was **demolished** several years ago.

8. **Solar energy** is still very expensive.

9. They must be **filthy** rich to have a house like that.[1]

10. Do you think we ought to **limit** the amount of electricity we use in our homes?

---

1. *Filthy rich* is idiomatic. Literally, *filthy* means very dirty.

D. Prepositions and Verb-Completers: Write any appropriate preposition or verb-completer in the blank spaces.

1. This is a description _____ life _____ fuel.

2. Subway trains will be broken down one morning _____ _____ every five mornings _____ 1997.

3. You will be lucky if you have a job _____ demolition.

4. First, the price _____ gasoline went way _____ .

5. There will be some advantages _____ 1997.

6. The conditions are worse _____ the suburbs than _____ the cities.

7. What energy is left is saved _____ agriculture.

8. The difficulty _____ distribution _____ food forces people _____ eat less.

9. The rest _____ the world is not as lucky as the United States.

10. What can we do _____ prevent all this now?

E. Cloze Exercise: Fill in the blanks with any appropriate word.

It's 1997, and it's raining, _____ you'll have to walk to
       (1)
_____ again. Any given subway train _____ down one
  (2)   (3)
morning out of _____ . The buses are gone, and _____ a
                   (4)   (5)
day like today, bicycles slosh _____ slide.
                                   (6)

Lucky you have a _____ in demolition. It's slow and
                      (7)
_____ work, but steady. The fading structures _____ a
    (8)   (9)
decaying city are the _____ mineral mines and hardware shops
                          (10)
_____ the nation.
    (11)

F. **Punctuation Exercise: Write in capital letters, periods, and commas where needed.**

anyone older than ten can remember automobiles at first the price of gasoline climbed—way up finally only the well-to-do drove and that was too clear an indication that they were filthy rich so any automobile on a city street was overturned and burned the cars vanished becoming part of the metal resource

G. **Word Forms: Choose the correct word form to fit into each sentence. Use appropriate verb tenses, singular or plural forms for nouns, and passive voice where necessary.**

1. **restriction, to restrict, restrictive**
   a. This regulation is too _____ . I think it should be changed.
   b. Fuel oil use will have to be _____ if the supply continues to decrease.
   c. Are there any _____ regarding the use of fuel oil now?

2. **crowd, to crowd, crowded**
   a. There is a huge _____ gathered around the entrance to the theater.
   b. Please don't _____ . There is room for everybody.
   c. I left because the room was too _____ and smoky.

3. **heating, heater, heat, to heat, hot, heated, hotly, heatedly**
   a. The weather is very _____ today.
   b. Would you please turn down the _____ ? It's too hot in here.
   c. How do you _____ your house in the winter?
   d. It was a very _____ argument.
   e. She responded _____ to his accusations.
   f. Do you have central _____ ?
   g. I have an electric _____ .

4. **convenience, to inconvenience, convenient, conveniently**
   a. Is May the 22nd _____ for you?
   b. Please set a time of your _____ .
   c. My apartment is _____ close to my job, so I walk to work.
   d. Please don't _____ yourself. I know how busy you are.

5. **luck, lucky, luckily**
   a. He's a _____ person.
   b. Do you usually have good _____ ?
   c. _____ , I had enough money to pay the bill.

6. **maintenance, to maintain**
   a. How much does it cost to _____ your car per year?
   b. Does your car require a lot of _____ ?

7. **fear, to fear, fearful, fearless, fearfully, fearlessly**
   a. I _____ the news is bad.
   b. I was feeling _____ because I kept hearing strange noises coming from the other room.
   c. Do you have any unusual _____ ?
   d. The child looked at his mother _____ when he heard the loud noise.
   e. She swam out into the ocean _____ .
   f. She has a _____ personality; she's ready to try anything.

8. **ease, to ease, easy, easily**
   a. They solved the problem with _____ .
   b. I _____ myself out of the room before he recognized me.
   c. This problem is _____ .
   d. You can solve it _____ .

9. **imagination, to imagine, imaginative, imaginatively**
   a. Her writing is full of _____ and humor.
   b. Can you _____ how much fun it was?
   c. He's very _____ , so I'm sure he will be able to give us some good ideas.
   d. The room was decorated very _____ .

10. **use, to use, useful, useless, usefully, uselessly**
    a. That information is interesting, but is it _____ ?
    b. You are welcome to have it if you can _____ it.
    c. The _____ of this tool is unclear.
    d. He was _____ employed, and he enjoyed his work.
    e. Don't keep arguing about it _____ ; just forget it, and go on to something else.
    f. This report is _____ ; it has no new or relevant information in it.

H. Sentence Scramble: Make a sentence out of each group of words.

1. without – life – unpleasant – would – be – fuel – very
2. winter – cold – homes – be – would – in
3. few – cars – there – be – would – very
4. however – pollution – there – be – less – would
5. fewer – also – crimes – would – be – there

I. Topics for Discussion and Composition:

1. Isaac Asimov paints a pessimistic view of life in 1997. As he admits, this "is a picture of the worst, of waste continuing, of oil running out, of nothing in its place, of world population continuing to rise." Do you agree with Asimov's gloomy prediction? If so, why? If not, why not? Please give at least three reasons to support your position and give specific examples to develop your reasons. You may take examples from this article if you wish.

2. Pretend that you are a child living in the year 1997 and that conditions are similar to those described in "Life without Fuel." Write about a typical day in your life.

3. Pretend that you are a grandparent in the year 1997 and that you are describing life in the old days (before the fuel ran out) to your grandchildren. Emphasize the unusual features of life in the old days.

4. Not all futurists (people who study the future) agree with Asimov's gloomy predictions. Many futurists believe that people will solve the most urgent problems facing them now and that life in the future will be at least as good, if not better, than it is today. What do you believe about the future? Will people solve their most urgent living problems? Please define these problems and tell how people might solve them.

5. Compare life now with life twenty years ago. Do you think life is better now than it was then? Why? Or why not? Please give several reasons for your position and give specific examples to support your reasons.

6. What is the single most urgent problem facing people in the future? Why? Please give several reasons why this is the most serious problem and give specific examples to support your reasons.

J. Reading Reconstruction: Read this paragraph as many times as you can in three minutes. Then, with your book closed, try to restate the ideas as clearly and completely as you can. (See Chapter I exercise for complete instructions.)

Life in 1997

Hello. My name is Lara, and I want to tell you about my life. It is 1997 now, and I am nine years old. I live in a small city, and my father and mother ride bicycles to work. We have a garden, and we grow almost all of our vegetables. There are community gardens in every neighborhood also. These gardens used to be parking lots, but now there are almost no cars, so this land is used for gardens. The air is much cleaner now than it used to be according to my parents. They tell me that the cars caused a lot of pollution in the old days. Also my parents say that children are healthier now than they used to be. They play outside more, and they don't watch television as much. Most people don't even have televisions and the ones who do watch only for a short time each day because electricity is carefully restricted. We do not have central heating, but we stay warm enough in the winter because we dress warmly in the house. In general, I think that our life is healthy and good. I am sure that children have as much fun now as they ever did—maybe more! Who knows?

Key words (to be written on the chalkboard):

bicycles	parking lots	electricity
vegetables	pollution	restricted
community	healthier	central heating
neighborhood		

K. Comprehension Check: On a separate piece of paper, write the numbers 1 through 10 on both sides. Mark one side "Test 1" and the other side "Test 2." Read each statement and decide whether it is true or false. Write "T" after true statements and "F" after false statements under Test 1. After you have finished the comprehension check, turn Test 1 face down. Then read the article again and do the comprehension check again under Test 2. Base your answers on the information in this article *only*, even if you disagree with what the author said.

1. According to this article, public transportation will be much better in 1997 than it is now.

2. According to this article, there will be fewer cars in 1997 than now.

3. Air will be cleaner in 1997.

4. The crime rate will be higher.

5. All homes will have central heating and air conditioning.

6. People will dress warmly indoors to try to keep warm in winter.

7. Conditions will be worse in the suburbs than in the cities.

8. The big problem in the suburbs will be getting and distributing food.

9. The United States will be in better condition than most other countries around the world in 1997.

10. This is an imaginary picture of life without fuel.

Review Examination III (Chapters 9, 10, 11, 12)

A. Prepositions and Verb-Completers: Write any appropriate preposition or verb-completer in the blank spaces. (20 points: 1 point each.)

1. Men are now working _____ a wide variety _____ jobs once held nearly exclusively _____ women.

2. The males _____ female-dominated fields may be making life easier _____ the women too.

3. Stress is not new; cave men suffered _____ stress too.

4. They worried _____ being eaten _____ a bear or dying _____ hunger.

5. People can learn how _____ cope _____ stress.

6. Everyone was very excited _____ the successful mission _____ the spaceship, the Columbia.

7. This was the first time that a spacecraft had been successfully landed _____ _____ earth _____ a space voyage.

8. Life _____ fuel will not be pleasant.

9. However, there will be some advantages _____ 1997.

10. The conditions will be worse _____ the suburbs than _____ the cities.

B. Word Forms: Look at the first word in each line. Write the appropriate form of this word in the sentence that follows it. Be careful to use appropriate verb tenses, singular and plural forms for nouns, and passive voice where necessary. (50 points: 2 points each.)

(Example)

live: ____*Life*____ without fuel will not be pleasant.

1. **train:**   Where did you receive your medical _____ ?

2. **enroll:**   What is the _____ at your school?

3. **ridicule:**   Don't be _____ .

4. **employer:**   John _____ here for four years.

5. **encourage:**   That is very _____ news.

6. **understanding:**   I don't _____ what you are doing.

7. **respond:**   Speak up so that we can hear your _____ .

8. **definite:**   Please look the _____ up in your dictionary.

9. **basis:**   _____ , that's the whole plan.

10. **relation:**   People say we look alike, but we are not_____ .

11. **energy:**   Children are usually very _____ .

12. **success:**   She's a _____ lawyer.

13. **invest:**   The project sounds interesting, but I am certain that it will require a large _____ .

14. **immediate:**   Please respond _____ .

15. **expense:**   I bought the most _____ watch.

16. **socialize:**   Don't you think that _____ programs are important?

17. **beneficial:**   Who will _____ from this program?

18. **heater:**   Please open the window. It's too _____ in here.

19. **crowded:**   Don't _____ together so closely.

20. **convenience:**   Unfortunately, that is not a _____ time for me.

21. **use:**   Thank you. I am sure the information will be very _____ .

22. **ease:**   She won the race _____ .

23. **imagine:**   His stories were wonderful because he has a fine _____ .

24. **fearful:**   You have nothing to _____ but fear itself.

25. **stress:**   Let me _____ again the importance of handling this situation carefully.

C. **Synonyms: From this list choose a synonym for the word in bold type in the sentences below. (20 points: 2 points each.)**

control	outspoken	possibility
very large	too much	it takes a lot of time
to handle	preference	doesn't have enough money
survive		

1. Do you think we should give **priority** to that program?

2. The proposed budget is **huge.**

3. Men tend to be more **assertive** than women do at work.

4. **It's very time-consuming** to check those statistics.

5. The **potential** for advancement is good.

6. She **can't afford** to buy a new car; so she's buying a used one.

7. How long will we **last** without oil?

8. **Excessive** stress is not good for you.

9. It's important to learn how **to cope with** stress.

10. We should try to **limit** the amount of electricity we use.

D. **Cloze: Please fill in the blanks with any appropriate word. (10 points: 1 point each.)**

First of all, I _____ to make it clear _____ I am not
                  (1)   (2)
against the space _____ . I just think it costs _____ much
                        (3)   (4)
and that society _____ benefit more from improved social
                      (5)
_____ than from space exploration. _____ we could have
   (6)   (7)
both— _____ elaborate space program and _____ good
         (8)   (9)
social welfare programs— _____ would be very happy.
                          (10)

CREDITS

Tribalism Is Important in Africa. © 1977 by the Los Angeles Times. This article has been edited and rewritten for this textbook. Photographs: UNICEF photos by (1) Peter Larsen; (2) M.&.F. Bernheim.

The Earth's Spreading Deserts. © 1981 by Hirasawa and Markstein. Reprinted by permission. Photographs reprinted with permission of United Nations.

Living a Long Life. © 1981 by Hirasawa and Markstein. Reprinted by permission. Photograph reprinted with permission of Black Star, from Family Circle, "The Long Life Diet," August 23, 1977.

The Female Mosquito. © 1981 by Markstein and Hirasawa. Reprinted by permission. Illustration reprinted by permission of the University of California Press © 1955.

Test Your Nutrition IQ. © 1977 by Consumers Union of the United States, Inc., Mt. Vernon, NY 10550. Adapted by permission from CONSUMER REPORTS, February 1977. Photograph: "It's delicious, but is it nutritious?" by Dorien Grunbaum.

Mexico's Passionate Affair with the Comics by Alan Riding. © 1977 by the New York Times Company. Reprinted by permission. Photographs courtesy of New York Times Pictures.

Marriage Advertising in India's Sunday Newspapers by William Borders. © 1977 by the New York Times Company. Reprinted by permission.

Exploding the Myths About the American Family by Earl C. Gottschalk, Jr. Reprinted from the December 13, 1977 issue of Family Circle Magazine. © 1977 THE FAMILY CIRCLE, INC. Photograph courtesy of J. Kilgore.

Women's Work? by Carol Hymowitz. Reprinted by permission of The Wall Street Journal. © Dow Jones & Company, Inc., 1981. All rights reserved. Photograph: "When I grow up, I want to be a nurse—just like my dad" by Dorien Grunbaum.